Natalie Bennett, or Baroness Benr
occasions, is one of two Green Part
was the leader of the Green Party c ......gland and Wales from 2012–16,
when she led the party to its best-ever election result, with more votes
than in every previous general election added together. She spent twenty
years as a journalist, from newspapers in the Australian countryside,
through the *Bangkok Post* to *The Times*, finishing as editor of the *Guardian
Weekly*.

Substack: nataliebennett.substack.com
X: @natalieben
Facebook: GreenNatalieBennett
Instagram: GreenNatalieBennett
TikTok: nataliebennettgreen

With special thanks to the super patrons of
Change Everything:

Andy Fewings

Interaction Design Studio – Diarmad McNally

CHANGE EVERYTHING

How we can rethink, repair and rebuild society

Natalie Bennett

Dear Kate,

Very best wishes

First published in 2024

Unbound
c/o TC Group, 6th Floor King's House, 9–10 Haymarket, London SW1Y 4BP
www.unbound.com

Typeset by Jouve (UK), Milton Keynes

A CIP record for this book is available from the British Library

ISBN 978-1-80018-302-5 (paperback)
ISBN 978-1-80018-303-2 (ebook)

Printed in Great Britain by Clays Ltd, Elcograf S.p.A

MIX
Paper | Supporting
responsible forestry
FSC® C018072

For Mum

With thanks to the patrons of *Change Everything*:

Professor Debbie Bartlett
Mr Brett David Bennett BA(Hons) MA FRSA
Paul Dawson
Jan Grothusen
Jack Lenox
Richard Mallender
Joanne Merrison
Tim Weller

Contents

Introduction
The World We Have Made

What has been called political common sense over recent decades – that greed is good, inequality does not matter, and we can keep treating the planet as a mine and a dumping ground – has been proved to be the exact opposite. It has been a recipe for disaster. This so-called common sense – in fact the ideology of neoliberalism – has delivered poverty and destruction, with a few benefitting while the rest of us pay. The centrist approach of leaving the UK, or the world, continuing to run as it does now, with just a few minor adjustments to the levers, a twirl of a policy dial here, a nudge of a management system there, is clearly not viable. Going further on our current path is even more disastrous.

The climate has been wrenched out of the Holocene*

---

* The Holocene is the geological period that began about 11,700 years ago, at the end of the last ice age. The Anthropocene is a term that has come to be widely used this century, defining a new geological epoch in which human activities have changed the Earth's geology and ecosystems. There is a huge debate about when it should start, and suggestions of alternative terms, such as 'Capitalocene' (referring to the effects of capitalism), and Donna Haraway's Chthulucene. I use Anthropocene as the most known term, and will go with the Anthropocene Working Group of the International Commission on Stratigraphy's 1950 start date.

stability in which our societies developed, into the radical uncertainty of the Anthropocene, in which our actions determine our own fate. Multinationals continue to hunt for new oil and gas fields, mining companies eye the deep ocean floor, and industrial agriculture slashes away at the Amazon as the sixth mass extinction[1] gathers pace. Half the mass of plants that were on the planet have gone,[2] only a sixth of the wild animals remain, while domesticated pigs and cows, kept often in conditions that can only be described as torture, make up nearly half of the mass of mammals.[3] Domestic poultry totals three times the mass of wild birds.[4]

Despite all of this abusive overproduction, more than 800 million people regularly go to bed hungry, but their number is far over-matched by the number ill from obesity.[5] Behind the latter is multinational companies pushing ultra-processed food-like substances sold wrapped in multiple layers of the single-use plastic that is choking the planet. Billionaires' bank balances balloon beyond what even the fanciest superyacht could consume, while the poor are forced to struggle for a pittance, treated with disrespect as 'unskilled labour' as even the professionally qualified are increasingly commodified.

Many draw parallels with the 1930s, before the world was engulfed in the cataclysm of global war, with the rise of far-right leaders in Hungary, Poland, Italy, the UK and beyond, and looming threateningly in the US and France. That far-right politics is grounded in fear. It holds that this is a difficult, dangerous, limited world in which survival demands grabbing what we can for 'us' and 'ours', snatching it from the hands of others, building walls to keep 'them' out. It tells people they are weak and powerless, that they need a 'strong leader' to ride up on a white horse to rescue them. All they have to do is follow along obediently.

A vision of hope

Standing against far-right politics is its direct opposite, based on sustainable, democratic sharing of the Earth's resources. This is the Green alternative. This is true common sense, building on the foundations of science, compassion and the human capacity to innovate. Green political philosophy believes in the power of human caring and creativity when freed from the deadening hand of our present oligarchy. It understands that there are enough resources on this fragile planet for all of us to have a decent life and for nature and climate to be restored – if we share them out fairly. It is grounded on people and communities making decisions for themselves, only sending power and resources upwards when absolutely necessary. This is a world of deliberative democracy, where citizens have the time and opportunity to inform themselves; to consider, debate with their fellows, and arrive at careful, balanced decisions about the allocation of resources and the division of powers. It is a world in which everyone is a leader.

When I speak, as I have several times a week over the past decade, to public and party meetings, to schoolchildren and university students, to community groups and workplaces, I aim to set out a vision of what that hopeful, caring, secure future looks like. I have heard those audiences' thoughts, seen their reactions to what they think will work, and what will not. And I have heard again and again, from very different people, that they had arrived at the meeting in despair and left with hope.

So that is what *Change Everything* aims to do – to set out a vision of hope, showing how we can innovate our way to freedom, prosperity, health and resilience. The book is not filled with discussion of hard-edged technology. It does not shine with solar panels and hum with electric cars. It does not talk about how society can be powered by smart grids and be comfortable in well-designed and -built structures fit for the new climate. All of those things are important and necessary, and there are lots of books about them, but their authors generally have a vision of a business-as-usual society with added technology. When I am talking about innovation, I mean something far more fundamental and transformative – innovation in the ways our societies work, how we care for each other, relate to each other and the natural world, and meet our most basic needs. And, crucially, how we think about our lives.

Back in 697 CE, the abbot Adomnán, the ninth abbot on the Scottish island of Iona, got the Synod of Birr to agree his 'Law of Innocents'. It has been described as the first Geneva Convention, directing that non-combatants should not only not be attacked, but be protected, during war. Thirteen hundred years on, our physical technologies would be incomprehensible to the pioneering abbot, but we are still trying to deliver the basic human rights – protection from war and violence, but also from want and fear, the social innovation that he saw so clearly was needed. As societies, as a species, our development has been grossly unbalanced towards technological innovation, while social change has stalled. That has to change.

Far beyond Beveridge

This is a transformation on an even greater scale than we saw in the UK after the Second World War, when there was an acknowledgement, at least for some,* that the sacrifices of millions in wartime had to be repaid with security, health and prosperity. The 1942 Beveridge Report promised to deliver the nation from disease, ignorance, squalor and idleness. That ushered in a period that some economists call the Great Levelling, a slow but steady reduction in inequality in the UK. The US, more weakly, took a similar direction. A mixed economy in the UK under the umbrella of social democracy saw Conservatives comfortable with state ownership of coal mines and car factories, and even railways. There was a general acceptance of the need for a 'family wage', enough for a man (this was a period of extraordinarily rigid gender roles) to support a wife and a couple of children. A London postman had a steady job and income. He could expect to pay off a good-sized house with garden over his working life, on that single wage.

That social democratic consensus lasted for three decades, until a series of global economic shocks – and perhaps a sense

---

* I say some, for many who served the war effort, who saw themselves as citizens of empire, from the Indian subcontinent and the Caribbean, were pushed off 'home' just as fast as the authorities could manage. Others who had loyally served the cause, like 2,000 Chinese seamen, many of whom were married to English women, were forcibly deported at zero notice, in an early, and utterly disgraceful example of the continuing racist 'Hostile Environment'.

of tiredness, of a failure to be able to imagine further advancement – opened the space for a new transformation. It has been called neoliberalism, Thatcherism and neo-Thatcherism (or Reaganism in the US). That was the ruling consensus, what you had to embrace to be called part of the political mainstream in the eighties, nineties and noughties. It celebrated greed as a positive force, believed that prosperity could flood to the top of society and then 'trickle down' to the rest, and that anything run by the public sector had to be sclerotic and wasteful, so anything operated for profit was preferable.

The fantasy of 'progress'

After three decades of dominance, neoliberalism was clearly running out of steam when I joined the Green Party on 1 January 2006. It was my New Year's pledge to do something about the economic, environmental and education systems that were clearly failing us all, the decision underpinned by a sense of deep unease. I felt that the state of the world – environmentally, economically, socially – was dangerously unstable, lacking in resilience for the challenges ahead. I am not claiming to have predicted the 2007–8 financial crash, the Brexit/Trump/Johnson political train wreck, or even to have grasped just how fast the warming world would burst into flames. Rather, I had not forgotten the lessons from an agricultural science degree completed in Australia decades earlier: that the world's soils were being mined and poisoned rather than cared for. I had studied enough history – from the Indian subcontinent to the Eastern Romans – to have a healthy doubt about narratives of continual progress. And after nearly a quarter-century as a journalist – having watched the Asian financial crash of 1997 from a front-row seat in Bangkok and ridden through the London property boom of the noughties – I knew well that our current economic structures were profoundly unstable.

But what I found, as I started door-knocking in North London with the Green Party, was that my unease was not widely shared. Householders sat back in their armchairs, waved a hand dismissively, and said, 'Well, sure, the grandkids will have to worry about climate change, but we will have plenty of money to do that. Gordon Brown has abolished boom and bust, and we will sail as a nation onto the sunny uplands of endless prosperity on the backs of a few clever bankers in the City.' The infamous narrative of the then chancellor's Mansion House speech in June of that year did not originate with him – it reflected what was seen as common sense.[6]

Letting in fresh air

Then came the 2007–8 financial crash, and many of those highly bonused, apparently clever people were pictured emerging from shiny office blocks clutching hastily grabbed items thrust into cardboard boxes. They were refugees from hubris, their too-clever-by-half financial instruments the cause of their institutions' destruction. Those on the left of politics saw this as their chance. The Overton window – the space in which mainstream politics could be conducted – had been dragged far to the right by Margaret Thatcher, being followed by her political child, Tony Blair. Now was the chance to get issues of poverty, inequality, community destruction in what's now called the 'Red Wall', and even environmental issues, back onto the mainstream agenda.

But the Overton window did not immediately shift left; it moved even further to the right. Old Etonian and Oxbridge man David Cameron was elected prime minister, the political child of Blair in his embrace of socially liberal causes such as equal marriage, but also in his belief that the bankers were the way out of the economic mess. The poor, the disadvantaged and the young would have to pay for the recovery through austerity's slashing of public services, the massive hiking of student fees and the further selling-off of every bit of the national silver that the previous Labour government had not managed to flog. The NHS was further handed over to US private health interests, free schools smoothly developed from Labour's academies. Even the Queen's head on stamps, a privatisation too far for Thatcher, hit the auction block. Globally, the Copenhagen United Nations climate-change conference of 2009 – which I watched from a new place as editor of the *Guardian Weekly* – collapsed in acrimony. The climate crisis had popped its head into the public realm but was quickly squashed down as a luxury to be considered in better economic times.

The mainstream left of British politics was flailing. It did not disown the aged, always inaccurate model of the national budget as being like a household one. It did not offer economic change, just a slightly softened form of neoliberalism. Ed Miliband, then Labour Party leader, in the 2015 election sought to say as little as possible about anything in the hope that the keys to No. 10 would fall into his lap. They did not.

Back to the future is for the movies

The lack of ideas was not one person's responsibility: Labour after Blair genuinely did not have an alternative model to offer. All even the left of the party could come up with was to go back to a rose-coloured, marginally updated 1960s view of strong sectoral unions, wage councils and a bit of government spending on nuclear power stations and new roads. I remember sitting in the Unite the Union office on Euston Road around 2014, hearing talk of setting sectoral minimum wages while wondering just how website designers and freelance event organisers were going to fit into this model.

One of the problems of such arenas is that they draw on a very narrow group in society – an awful lot of whom have studied politics, philosophy and economics at Oxbridge. They read the same books, run in the same London circles. They rely on political philosophies a century or more old. You would not set out to operate in the modern world with an 1870s typewriter. Our physical technologies have moved on, but our social technologies – be it political systems or schools or economic arrangements – are stuck in the nineteenth century. Both the largest parties – but particularly the Labour Party – love to talk about 'hard-working families'. Yet we stopped sending children up chimneys and down mines a century ago.

They are wedded to the idea that what we have now is 'progress', that history had an inevitable course that was leading, through providence, even when the religious underpinnings fell away, to where we are today. 'The West' in the twentieth century was, not just for Francis Fukuyama with his 'end of history' thesis, the pinnacle of human development.[7] Karl Marx and traditional Liberals were also entirely wedded to this idea of progress in inevitable stages. If you dig into the assumptions of many politicians today, they are too. It is a racist and ridiculous view. (We might compare our 'success' in achieving 'civilisation' to the 50,000 years or more of continuous flourishing that Indigenous Australians achieved.) We once thought the same about biological evolution: think of those T-shirts that show knuckle-dragging apes standing up in stages to 'modern man'. (It always seems to be a man.) Science has discarded such myths; social theory and practical politics far too often have not.

Co-creating a new politics

In 2012 I was elected as leader of the Green Party of England and Wales, a post I served in for four years, which covered the period of the 'Green Surge'. On its busiest day more than 3,000 people joined the party. We got into the UK leadership debates for the first time, so I locked horns with David Cameron, Ed Miliband, Nick Clegg and Nigel Farage, while largely agreeing with Nicola Sturgeon and Leanne Wood. I was very glad they were there, because otherwise I would have been a lone anti-austerity voice. And I am proud that many girls and women have come up to me since and said how inspired they were to see an (almost) gender-balanced debate – and the fact that Nicola, Leanne and I hugged at the end of the second, leaving Nigel Farage out in the cold. Greens got more votes in that election than in every previous general election – but still only one MP. (Democracy – it would be a good idea.)

In those four years, and continuing since, I have spoken to many hundreds of groups of people, young and old, in every corner of these islands. A lunchtime student event at Teesside University, Middlesbrough was memorable for its intensity and length. I usually call 'time' on an event when I can see from the body language that the audience has had enough, but in Middlesbrough the questions, the passion, kept coming into the third hour. It was my energy that ran out before the audience's enthusiasm. I told a group of Year Fives and Sixes (aged ten and eleven) at Burley Oaks Primary School in Wharfedale, West Yorkshire, that they should make politics what they do, not have done to them – a message at the core of every meeting I do. Came the smart response: Had I done politics at their age? I had to ask myself, fast, why I had not. (My answer was that no one had told or shown me that people could get together to build change. Australia in the 1970s could not see beyond the individual. I tried on my own, but did not get far.) With Barnsley Skeptics in the Pub (a group operating around the country that does great work in promoting scientific and political debate), I heard from a recently retired man who said he now had no idea how he had managed to find the time for a job. His life was now full with minding the grandkids, running the local supportive community combining practical work and companionship (Men in Sheds), his allotment and his friends. His comments helped grow my understanding of universal basic income (see Chapter 1).

Many ideas and arguments in this book have been inspired by inputs like those from all around the country, from people of different ages and backgrounds. Every idea in this book has been road-tested in these discussions, honed by interaction. We can only get through this dangerous stage of the development of *Homo sapiens* by relying on the collective ingenuity, talent and creativity of millions of people, all empowered to 'do politics', all being heard. This book aims to synthesise the voices I have heard – and encourage them to step forward. They collectively represent true common sense.

That is why I chose to publish through crowdfunding, an approach that provided a huge percentage of the resource for the Green Party's 2015 election campaign. It is democratic publishing – increasingly also a route for funding academic research and the creative sector. This acts as a reminder that for all the complaints about the political impacts of social media, it can be used for good, since that is generally how the word gets out to prospective supporters. In early modern times authors had to secure the patronage of the great and the good – royalty and aristocracy – to get into print. Now, anyone with £10 to spare can help the ideas of others spread – and can see themselves reflected back.

To everyone who has contributed, I say: *thank you*. These are people doing politics in their daily lives: in their actions, in their thinking. Their common-sense politics bears little resemblance to what you hear in Westminster, the parliamentary chambers or the television studios. It is focused on the reality of everyday lives, the physical limits of the planet, the enormous public health issues our society faces.

Their thinking – and mine – collectively challenges three key ideas that the neoliberal and social democratic visions of society share in their narrow, so similar, understandings of the world.

Fallacy 1: We need economic growth

'Mainstream' politics sees economic growth as essential to keep our economic and social systems afloat. As the *Financial Times* pointed out in 2017, two such disparate politicians as Theresa May and Jeremy Corbyn shared the belief in the need for growth; they just wanted to distribute the proceeds differently.[8] Yet you cannot have infinite growth on a finite planet. That is an old Green saying, and also a fundamental truth. We are beyond six of nine of Earth's planetary boundaries – climate, biodiversity, flows of phosphorus and nitrogen, creation of novel entities (the 'Three Ps': plastics, pesticides and pharmaceuticals), ocean acidification and freshwater use.[9]

Kate Raworth in the brilliant *Doughnut Economics* sets out the rethinking this demands very clearly. In his widely read *Prosperity Without Growth*, Tim Jackson focused on the climate element, demonstrating that you can reduce the carbon intensity of growth, but not decouple the link between growing Gross Domestic Product (GDP) and carbon emissions.

The concept of 'needing' growth is based on the metaphor that this is a pie which has to keep growing, so that all keep getting more even while their share remains the same – even if for many that only means a few more crumbs. But what we have to do instead is maintain the size of the pie – within the planet's limits – and slice it up fairly. Neither neoliberalism nor social democracy can cope with that.

Fallacy 2: You must have 'a job'

The second way in which social democracy and neoliberalism are alike is that both see the way in which an individual finds a place in society is through a job: a defined, paid role in an organised place of work that provides the majority of your income. I will never hear the name Rachel Reeves (current Labour shadow chancellor) without thinking of her declaration for the Labour Party that: 'We are not the party of people on benefits. We do not want to be seen, and we're not the party to represent those who are out of work.'[10] Like Bill Clinton in America, Tony Blair saw the answer to social problems as getting more and more people into 'jobs'. In the ideal world of this model, coupled parents would both be in paid employment, and in the unfortunate case of single mothers, they would be pushed out into the workplace as soon as humanly possible. Work was supposed to pay, and if it did not, that was the fault of the individual, not the system. In 2024, with a Conservative government forced to acknowledge that many jobs do not provide enough money to live on, their answer is that people should upskill and find a better-paid job, ignoring the fact that many of the lowest-paid jobs, from social care to delivering parcels, are the most essential of all.

'A job' is where social identity is situated and worth allocated, in this view. That has always been a problem for women. In the world of social democracy, the one I grew up with in an attenuated form in Australia, my mother and her friends, without irony or anger, would apologetically say they were 'just a housewife'. That was not seen as a job; it did not generate an income. It was not valued, and the people who did it were also not valued. That they not only raised the children and cared for the elders, but also ran the parents' and friends association that kept the school budget afloat, and tended the needs of men battered, mentally and sometimes physically, in the workplace, was not regarded as a 'job', so they were not seen to deserve respect. This is the sixties American feminist Betty Friedan's 'problem that has no name' (the subtitle of her 1963 book *The Feminine Mystique*), from which we have still not escaped.

In the neoliberal age, that traditionally female caring role became even less valued. The 'welfare mum' became a figure of abuse and distrust, viewed as a subject to be forced into paid employment as soon as possible. Every rise in the percentage of the working-age population in jobs was cause for celebration, a gain for 'equality'. It is telling that it is in access to employment – where more labour was needed for 'the economy' – that the women's movement made the most progress.

Yet finding identity and security through paid work has run into a dead end. First, work, more and more, does not pay. Nearly half of working-age adults receiving benefits in the UK today are in work, but they cannot get sufficient funds, or enough hours, from that work – very often a zero-hours contract – to meet the needs that even the government is prepared to acknowledge are necessary. Secondly, to find work, in many fields and many parts of the country, workers have to make their own job (or create one or more side hustles to supplement their 'job'). That is true across the creative sector, and in many poorer regions of Wales, where virtually everyone I have met had created their own business, often with a couple of side hustles added on, and so scraped together a living. In other fields, young people can expect to have to complete several years of unpaid, so self-funded, internships before any hope of employment is likely to emerge. Simply applying for a job – as I was lucky enough to do as a young graduate seeking my first job in journalism without any professional training in 1980s Australia – getting it, then building a career, is no longer feasible. Not to mention the fact that entire fields appear and disappear within a decade.

Fallacy 3: You have got to compete to get ahead

This is an idea now wired into international relations and economic theory: if you beat down the other nation, the other company, the other person, and grab what they have got, you will be better off. Call it the Genghis Khan theory of politics. As Greens we know that international relations, as with interpersonal, is not a zero-sum game. A secure world in which everyone has enough is a stable world; a society that works co-operatively to tackle its problems is far better off than one where a few are seeking to grab as much as they can while impoverishing the rest. If we work together to allow nature to flourish, rather than allowing commercial interests to subjugate it to their profit, we will have a far healthier world.

Both neoliberalism and social democracy focus on individual 'aspiration', each person seeking to leap ahead of their fellows, and the idea that the lack of it is what holds communities and individuals back. I had to hold my temper very firmly in check when I heard Stella Creasy, Labour MP for Walthamstow in East London, one of my early London stomping grounds, say that what her constituents needed was more aspiration. I had recently been with some of them – students of journalism at the University of East London. They were bursting with aspiration, wanting to know from me how they might get into national television, or the biggest magazines, or even a national newspaper. But I had to try to tell them, gently, that they did not have a hope in Hades: those jobs these days almost only ever go to someone whose parent, aunt or uncle works there, or who knows someone who does.

And 'aspiration' is explicitly built on the idea of a few individuals getting out of a disadvantaged community – moving up into a middle-class world and leaving their peers, parents and siblings behind. The Green alternative vision is a world in which every job is valued, respected and decently paid. We need school-dinner servers, bin collectors, bus drivers and bricklayers, and everyone occupying those roles should be respected and their labour properly valued. Then people can truly choose what they want to do with their life, develop their skills and talents as they wish. And choose, if they wish, to remain in the community that they first called home, not be sucked off to a big city.

System change: You do not build a wall with a sledgehammer

I am not a believer in perfect cycles of history. But it is clear that neoliberalism has run out of steam, as social democracy ran out of energy before it, without answers to the pressing problems – environmental, economic and social – of today.

That is not surprising, for both systems created many of our current crises. You do not fix problems with the tools that created them in the first place. The common chant on many demonstrations I attend is 'system change not climate change' – but that is just one reason to rethink and rebuild. It is people who need a new system, every bit as much as the planet does.

A completely new economic and social system must be built afresh, abandoning the three broken pillars of growth, the jobs economy, and competition. Green political philosophy, as outlined in this book, is built on the security of a universal basic income, the chance to flourish for every individual in a society that values all contributions. It understands the need for genuine lifelong learning opportunities, demands the establishment of genuine democracy, starting at the most local level, and works for the delivery of an international rights system whose norms have already been established by decades of campaigning. What it offers reflects the models, ideas and experiences of individuals and communities around these islands and beyond – including Transition Towns groups* and tenants' unions, repair cafés and Incredible Edible,† Occupy campaigners and climate strikers, community energy co-operatives and local food-growing schemes, volunteer nappy libraries and flatpack

---

* A now global 'movement of communities coming together to reimagine and rebuild our world' that began in Totnes, Devon, in 2006: transition-network.org/

† A movement that started with growing food in community spaces in the West Yorkshire town of Todmorden, which now has groups around the world: www.incredibleedible.org.uk/

democracy groups, Universal Basic Income Labs and new unions organising zero-hours contract workers.

History is not pre-written; it is made

When I speak at public meetings and focus on hope, I am often challenged about how I can hold on to that in a world where enormous power is in the hands of the status quo. How do I know our side will win, rather than the far right? For the rise of those malignant forces has been the dominant narrative of the past decade, told and retold in our media and worried over in our parliaments. There is good reason why the words of Antonio Gramsci, the Italian Marxist philosopher jailed by the fascists in 1926, are so often quoted now: 'The crisis consists precisely in the fact that the old is dying and the new cannot be born; in this interregnum a great variety of morbid symptoms appear.'

I do not know that we will win. There is no doubt those symptoms are dangerous. What I do know is that history is not pre-written or pre-ordained. It is made. And what makes it are the actions of individuals and groups, people getting together to do politics. And by that I do not only mean voting, campaigning in elections, standing for office and making decisions in councils or Parliament – as much as I want to encourage far greater involvement in all of those things. By politics I mean a class of children in a school deciding they want to get rid of the plastic cutlery in the canteen, and campaigning to make that happen. Or residents of a street organising a litter pick to clear up a piece of 'waste' ground, then inviting in the guerrilla gardeners to make it flower. Or a group of bicycle couriers getting together (as I saw such underpaid pieceworkers do in London a few years ago) to demand decent reward for their work and greater security in their lives.

What gets people involved, engaged and active is hope. Being told the rich will just keep getting richer as the poor get poorer, the world hotter and the ecosystems more and more depleted, until we collapse into misery and destruction, does not get people bouncing out of bed, eager to greet the day. Understanding that they can make a difference, improve their lives and those of others, save wildlife and get flowers growing – that is energising and exciting. It is empowering. And that is the last thing the far right want to see. That is one reason, among many, to ensure that hope is spread far and wide, exciting possibilities for the future are discussed, shaped into policies, and delivered, with full, deliberative democratic involvement. Promoting *doing politics* is the purpose of this book.

A thought experiment

This is a test I often invite audiences to engage in: imagine that we had created a wonderful society – similar to what it looked like we were heading for in the early 1960s. This is a society free from material want and insecurity, with great public infrastructure and secure, stable local economies. (And let's take it as read that we're also assuming we have moved on from 1960s awful gender relations and moral policing.) Lives are good, jobs are rewarding and respected, the future is bright. Then we discover the climate emergency.

The scientists tell us everything has to change. That would be *really* politically difficult.

The fact that we are in a social emergency, a political emergency, an economic emergency, is, in terms of delivering change, an opening. The status quo is profoundly unstable. Change is inevitable. That is good news. We are in a great position to build a better world.

Dystopic greenness

There is a flood of books offering 'Green alternatives' arriving now, from Bill Gates's naive *How to Avoid A Climate Disaster* to those that focus on individual and technological actions that can only scratch at the edges of the problem, like Mike Berners-Lee's *There is No Planet B*. They usually have chapters about shifting our energy system to renewable energy, technological change in transport, transforming our buildings with energy efficiency, different ways to use the land and produce our food, cutting meat consumption, and recycling. (Reminder: recycling is a poor third option behind reducing resource use and reusing the goods.)

Most Global North governments, and a good number in the Global South, have produced roadmaps for delivering such technological change. In the UK, the independent Climate Change Committee's carbon budgets a very clear and understandable job of setting out the changes needed so that even politicians can understand. But all of these plans, and many of these books, have a problem. A huge, insoluble in their own terms, problem. It is increasingly difficult to make the sums add up to keep global

warming below the 1.5°C above pre-industrial levels.*
That is if we assume that our society, our economies, our
lives, continue much as they are now, just with changes in
the physical fabric: 'business as usual with added technology'. That we rely on lots of solar panels and wind farms,
electric cars and home insulation, with a society arranged
essentially as it is now.

Yet that cannot be done. And so brand-new future technologies, including various forms of carbon capture and
storage, and scarily wild schemes for giant space mirrors and
floating seaweed continents, are fed in to try to make the
sums add up. Those visions have no more foundation than
the 1950s cartoons that suggested that by now we would all
be flying around cities in jet-propelled cars, swallowing
nutrition pills instead of meals, and jetting to Mars for our
holidays.

The argument of this book is that these visions are like a
one-legged stool that cannot even be made to precariously
balance. They are all built on hard technological innovation –
shiny metal machines built by multinational corporations
and white-coated lab scientists stirring up genetic cocktails.
These models assume that we will all continue to work
extraordinarily long hours, commute long distances, fly to

---

* The world is now at least 1.2°C above pre-industrial levels (the cyclical El
Nino weather system in the short term pushing us even higher), and the
degree of disorder and damage will only grow exponentially from here. At
the Paris climate talks in 2015, the agreement to aim for below 1.5°C was
seen as a sop thrown to the small island nations. Most climate and ecological scientists now see it as essential. That means a 'hard stop' of climate
emissions, starting now.

far-flung places in a desperate attempt to briefly escape the misery of our everyday lives, aim to have more stuff and consume more resources, and have no real say in the direction of our societies, which will be dictated by ever-more-dominant multinational companies. The hope of the neoliberals and the social democrats is that the pie will keep getting bigger so that even those many people only getting crumbs will get a few more crumbs.

Everyday politics

I have deliberately decided not to make this book 'philosophical' or technical. I do not explore how universal basic income might be seen to rebalance life between Hannah Arendt's ideas of 'work' and 'labour', or how it relates to Isiah Berlin's negative and positive liberty. I am not exploring some of the great ideas of various strands of ecofeminism, or ranging across an idea I have long embraced, Pierre Bourdieu's *habitus*. This book aims to use everyday language to entirely skip the jargonisation that has so consumed much of the humanities and social sciences.

I want it to be as accessible as possible, so this book is short. The Roman philosopher Cicero said: 'If I'd had more time I'd have written a shorter letter.' Boiling things down, getting in the essentials and little else, takes time and energy. My usual public meeting 'introduction to Green politics' talk of twenty minutes tends to extend to thirty when I am tired, and is not improved for it. In politics, there is always a desire to fit in one more argument, give one more example. But I know how my heart sinks when someone pulls out their

600-page report and says 'read this'. One of the books that has most influenced my political thinking is Stein Ringen's *Nation of Devils*, which covers a massive amount of ground on US, UK and global politics in 260 pages.

I want readers to go away and act – not be stuck for too long with me. So please enjoy the following pages; browse through them or skip through them; only read the bits that grab you if you like. Then go and *do* politics.

Part A

Active Freedom

Chapter 1

Decommodifying Time

In the Green future, you no longer work for 'the man'. You do not have to sell your labour to ensure you do not starve. You are not defined by a 'job'. There is universal basic income: you decide how to use your time, energy and talents.

'Security' is a word that needs to be liberated from right-wing usages. Security does not come from guns or missiles, or, most certainly, nuclear weapons. It starts with a world where everyone can put food on the table and keep a decent roof over their head. It means ensuring no one is left penniless and desperate. That starts with one foundational policy that tackles the pervasive insecurity that causes such damage to people and planet today, both in the UK – with the horror of Universal Credit and austerity, zero-hours contracts and rampant job insecurity – and around the globe: Universal Basic Income (UBI). The focus here is on how it could work in the UK, but trials in the Global South have demonstrated the transformative possibility of even a couple of dollars a day in secure income in many societies, not just for individuals but for whole communities.

Over the past centuries, food and shelter have been increasingly commodified, made part not of life but 'the economy'. In recent decades healthcare and social care have also been increasingly financialised. With the inclusion of more and more workers in 'the economy' – and if they are studying for longer, in the conventional view, that is just time spent preparing to enter 'the economy' – individuals' time and energy has been directed by bosses, not left under their own direction. A universal basic income decommodifies time. It takes back individual control and allows the hugely valuable resource to be put into building communities, restoring public health and repairing the natural world.

What is universal basic income?

A universal basic income is a payment made regularly to everyone accepted as a member of a society that meets their basic needs, for food, shelter, clothing and other essentials. It is universal because it goes to everyone, absolutely unconditionally. It cannot be taken away from you by the government. It does not diminish if you earn money, so there are no benefit traps as with Universal Credit, under which labour is 'rewarded' with loss of income and other supports. It is paid to individuals, not households, so everyone has money of their own – one reason why UBI is a profoundly feminist policy: our current system operates largely through households, which creates the potential for economic abuse, particularly of women.

This is a 'basic' payment because it is sufficient for the essentials. You can live a decent but not luxurious life on it, which distinguishes this from an idea sometimes promoted by the right wing that if you give everyone a little money, they can be forced to work for pittance wages. The assumption is that most people of working age will do at least some paid activities, or create things for which they will be paid, at least some of the time, but even without that, you will be sure of being able to put food on the table and keep a roof over your head. Children get a decent proportion of the adult total (paid to a parent or carer), people past working age a higher non-contributory pension that ensures they get access to a full life and the opportunities to continue to participate in society.

It is 'universal' because it is paid to everyone accepted as a member of a society. Beyond that, there are absolutely no conditions. That means it goes to millionaires and billionaires as well as everyone else. But the money comes back from them in taxes; it does not make them richer. And that lack of conditionality is crucial, making administration extraordinarily easy and cheap. Child benefits cost about 1 per cent of its total payout in administration (when it was universal) and UBI would be about the same.* The most basic level at which it can be set, as the Green Party has done in manifestos in 2015 and 2019, means the total cost is about double what benefits are now.

Even more crucially, it means no one misses out, as millions currently miss out on benefits to which they are entitled but have to apply for. That some 800,000 pensioners fail to get the pension credit to which they are entitled is just one demonstration of the reality of such conditional benefits: that many will be unable or unwilling to jump barriers (language, IT skills or pride) to get money they need.

---

* By contrast, the cost of delivering £1 of benefit now has been put at 28 pence: www.ubilabnetwork.org/blog/how-much-does-it-cost-to-give-someone-one-pound-in-benefits

Delivering security and cutting consumption

Bringing in a universal basic income has been the policy of the Green Party of England and Wales for more than four decades. One reason for that is environmental: insecurity drives a huge amount of consumption of this planet's desperately overtaxed resources. Houses in the UK are seen more as stores of cash than places to live; buying a bigger house, or another house, is one way of securing a retirement income not guaranteed by the state or the unstable financial sector. Fear of losing your job and being left penniless causes many to feel that they have to keep up with the Jones at the next desk by wearing the latest fashion or talking casually at the water cooler about their recent foreign weekend away. In our deeply unequal society, if you are not seen as a go-getter, you are at risk of being swept aside.

It is a pressure that has been added to (but not caused) by social media. Instagram influencers wearing a different outfit in every snap, swanning by a pool in Dubai even in the midst of a pandemic, are often attacked, but behind that is desperate insecurity, particularly for the young. That social media account is often needed for promotion of a professional career or as a side hustle to raise cash to cover the rent.

Green support for a universal basic income comes from another direction too, that of belief in the resources of our society being a 'commons', something of which everyone should have a share, just as the people of England once had a right to graze their livestock on common land and collect firewood from common woods, before enclosure took that away. The wealth of our society is built on endeavours by our ancestors (and an awful lot of pure, violent theft as well – see Chapter 12) and the collective efforts of us all today. We all contribute to build and maintain roads, schools, hospitals, libraries – all of the foundations on which businesses rely. It is common sense: if you put Elon Musk on a desert island, he would not be able to achieve anything at all. Businesses need customers, workers and infrastructure, from roads to internet links. Those are communal assets from which everyone should get a share of the returns.

Human rights and hunger

My path into conviction about the need for a universal basic income started with an exhibition at the British Library in 2008. 'Taking Liberties' looked back not only over the history of the struggle for human rights, but where it might lead in the future, making the point that the right to life demands the right to food, shelter and other essentials. Yet there is no nation in the world in which that is guaranteed. No country is on track to meet the Sustainable Development Goals the world agreed as a target for 2030. Only an unconditional universal basic income (set at a sufficient level) can guarantee the essentials. So arguing from the basic human right to life is usually where I start.

The arguments about insecurity driving consumption and the moral right to a share of the commons developed decades ago, in a more secure time, when poverty and inequality were falling, during the post-Second World War Great Levelling. As the neoliberalism of Margaret Thatcher and Ronald Reagan took hold, the number of reasons for having a UBI grew; the urgency became far greater. The impact of reduced welfare payments, low wages and spreading zero-hours contracts, and the axe of benefit sanctions, ensures many individuals now have no income at all. There are very few of us – perhaps only the 1 per cent of the richest – who can be sure that we will never be left penniless and desperate, and fear of that has pernicious impacts across society. We have essentially returned to the nineteenth century, when the threat of the debtors' prison loomed at the shoulder of even apparently prosperous families. As we increasingly understand that insecurity has extremely bad effects on physical and mental health, it is clear this is a significant factor in the epidemic of ill health that has swept across our societies.

There are also explicitly feminist arguments for a universal basic income. Most obviously, this is a feminist policy because it means no one can be trapped in an abusive relationship by lack of funds (an overwhelmingly gendered situation), but its feminism goes far further than that. It acknowledges that everyone in our society is contributing, but many of those contributions are not paid jobs: caring for the young and the old, running voluntary organisations, keeping an eye on the neighbourhood and managing its difficulties. These are all roles that have historically been, and continue to be, overwhelmingly occupied by women, and severely underacknowledged.

True democracy

I credit a seventeen-year-old Polish Green activist I met in Italy for pushing me towards further new thinking about how we promote and talk about universal basic income. He asked me how he could promote UBI in a society profoundly suspicious, for obvious historic reasons, of relying on the state for security, concerned about the power that could give the authorities. The argument that this would be a right that could not be taken away just did not cut it in these circumstances. In talking the problem through with him, it occurred to me that the claims we were making for UBI really were not large or broad enough. They failed to encompass its truly transformative potential.

The foundation of survival in a capitalist economy for the vast majority of individuals is using your time, energy and talents as directed by a boss – 'working for the man', as the great American twentieth-century musician Roy Orbison put it. Huge joint struggle through trade unions and by campaigners saw some restrictions put on bosses' control in much of the world. Children could not be forced to work. The hours worked each day were limited and weekends brought in.

Yet, astonishingly, the total hours worked in a year for those in full-time work has shifted little in a century. Socialist Robert Owen made the demand for what is still largely our standard day today in 1817: 'Eight hours' labour, eight hours' recreation, eight hours' rest.' (Being a man, and of his time, he did not consider the need for care: of children, of the elderly, of relationships.) But the UK opted out of elements of the EU Working Time Directive, even before Brexit, and communications technology has increasingly meant work never really stops. That is the very opposite of freedom. Add in commuting, essential self-maintenance and caring responsibilities, and for many people, particularly women, there is no recreation time left in the week.

In socialism, at least as delivered in the former Eastern

Bloc, it was the state that decided how you would use your time, energy and talents. That was the only way to security, and as in any situation where bosses and bureaucrats have directive power over workers' lives without effective controls or oversight, it was enormously open to abuse. You did not have to be in the gulag to face severe restrictions on your liberty, at least as the system developed. The Soviet Union did start with a principle of worker control over enterprises, but it was swept aside during Stalin's crash industrialisation drive. Women were forced into paid labour while nothing was done to relieve their domestic burden. Forced collectivisation took control of their working lives with relentless cruelty and great inefficiency.

True productivity

Given the foundation of a universal basic income to meet individual needs, people can make their own, truly free life choices to develop to their full potential, as precious few have the opportunity to do today. This is something I have long highlighted as a benefit of UBI. Think of the single parent who cannot now risk starting up the small business for which they have a brilliant idea because most small businesses fail, and even those that succeed usually have a highly variable income in the early years. It is very hard to risk your children going hungry. Or imagine the composer, poet or cabinetmaker who might produce a masterpiece, but who is instead condemned to employment in call-centre hell (which we all suffer with them whenever forced to deal with our bank or telecoms provider). With a universal basic income, they could use their skills and talents as they choose, use them well, rather than be forced to allow them to wither. If those hideous call centres cannot be staffed, we would have to find other – better – ways to provide services, such as local, physical offices.

I will admit that in a society with a UBI, you would probably get lots of really bad poetry written. But that would have an extremely low carbon footprint; you do not even have to print it if no one wants to read it. And if after a few years of trying to be a poet that did not work out, most people would head off to do something else. More positively, we'd get wonderful poetry written – and music composed, art created, and videos made, and new ideas for running society – that now have no hope of coming to life.

Yet it struck me, exploring this idea further, that the frame in which I was placing this idea of freedom was still too limited, too 'business-as-usual with added freedom'. I will excuse myself from one angle for my failure of imagination: one of the reasons why UBI has always spooked mainstream economists is trying to model what it would look like when people truly could decide for themselves how to spend their time – what would that magical beast 'the economy' look like under such conditions?

But given the state of the world today, in a pandemic that has accelerated and highlighted issues of poverty, inequality, insecurity and despair that were already deeply rooted, there is no excuse for timidity. We cannot continue as we are, and universal basic income – and the very different society it would bring – offers a way forward. For as anarchist political writer Emma Goldman said last century: 'No one is lazy. They grow hopeless from the misery of their present existence, and give up. Under our order of things, every man would do the work he liked, and would have as much as his neighbor, so could not be unhappy and discouraged.'[1]

Different ways of living that in some ways resemble what a UBI society might look like are being explored, informally, in our currently broken system. In the hybrid that is modern China, a mixture of capitalism and authoritarianism, the 'lying flat' movement led by its young people is seeking to develop a life as little involved in the rat race as possible. Recently in the West we have seen reports of the rise of 'hidden resignation', or 'quiet quitting' – employees doing what their contracts demand, but no more. Both can be seen as reaction against what social psychologist Devon Price has termed the 'laziness lie', which finds individual worth in productivity and tells individuals that there is always more they can be doing: no minute of the day is free, at least from guilt.

Jobs versus needs

An activist at the wonderful GalGael Trust in Glasgow* crystallised something I'd been thinking about for a long time. She said: 'In poor communities like this, there's no shortage of things that need doing, but precious few jobs.' Our current system ensures that most people of what we consider working age have little 'spare' time and energy. Consequently, many essential tasks are left undone.

In a universal-basic-income society, most people would

---

* I was told it started as an anti-road campaign seeking to protect a forest and has developed into a woodworking community centre that works particularly with people with drug, alcohol and mental health issues.

seek some paid work – it is, after all, a *basic* income – but the balance of that and community contribution could for many be turned around. And if you coordinated a community garden – say in the old car park of an abandoned supermarket – the produce would help ensure you do not need to buy much food. And your productivity, and contribution to society, would be far greater than when you were working as an administrator levying parking fines on that very same patch of land.

Genuine democracy

The universality of basic income means this freedom to use your time and energy as you choose is available not only to the few, of the 'right' gender, class, ethnicity or age, as 'freedom' has been in the past. Looking back in history, the Church of England reverend-cum-scientists, from author–naturalist Gilbert White to entomologist William Darwin Fox, relative and tutor of Charles Darwin, were in receipt of something very like a UBI – minimal demands in return for a secure income, the chance to use their time as they pleased. A secure, guaranteed income for all – not just a few middle- and upper-class men – could not just resurrect and create communities of scholars and craftspeople, carers and creatives, but be the basis of a nation, even a world, of them.

Being in control of your own time means being able to control both your outputs and your inputs; who would really want to labour in the early hours of the morning to produce dreadful sandwiches to be eaten in haste and misery by corporate slaves at their desks? It means being able to build your world. It has to be the foundation of anything really called democracy, which no country in the world has now. As Amelia Horgan wrote in *Lost in Work*: 'Work under capitalism is arranged, must be arranged, in such a way that workers do not have control over their work.' The trade union movement has – sometimes – focused on workplace democracy, and the idea of enterprises being co-operatives is an excellent one, but co-ops now are still operating within a model of most people 'having' to work. And what of people who do not have a paid, defined 'job' – how do they have a say in the economy under that model? They are truly powerless: ignored, refused even the most basic respect.

Tough jobs

One question often asked about society with a universal basic income is 'How will you get people to do the really horrible jobs?' My case study for this – because it resonates with most people – is sewer cleaners. Although at a public meeting when I used this example, an audience member put their hand up and said, 'My mate's a sewer cleaner and he loves his job.' Which makes sense, because doing something so obviously essential to the wellbeing of us all could indeed be rewarding. But maybe the public-service element would not be sufficient to attract enough people to be sewer cleaners (even when we have got rid of wet-wipe fatbergs by banning these disastrous products), so the pay would have to be good, really good. Which is fair enough, I would say. Probably the pay would be more than we would want or need to pay bankers. I say sewer cleaners *should* be paid more than bankers.

Living anywhere

'Levelling up' was the buzz phrase of Boris Johnson's government, forced to acknowledge the extreme levels of regional inequality in the UK. There was, however, no 'oven-ready' plan for tackling it, no real ideas at all. It was built on a false foundation, because the target was to make the rest of the country like London and the South-East, as though extending its economy, built on the Ponzi scheme that is the UK financial sector, was not both impossible and deeply undesirable. (London has some of the poorest parts of the country, lives blighted further by the cost of living in the capital.)

We should instead be thinking of spreading prosperity around these islands. And universal basic income is an ideal tool for that. All those hundreds of thousands of empty homes – particularly in the North – could be restored, repaired and communities revived by people on universal basic income. Of course there would be incomers – artists and musicians, activists and carers – but UBI would enable the many young people now forced to leave deprived coastal towns and rundown industrial centres to make a life for themselves in the communities they value as home. That would be restoration rather than gentrification.

People are a resource, not a problem

Politics in recent years has often been seen to be – particularly in the hands of the populists and the politicians who have tried to seduce their voters – mostly about migration. 'They are coming here taking *our* jobs.' (While also often, it has been claimed, arriving just for *our* welfare benefits – the contradictory nature of those two propositions not being challenged.) And the aim of 'creating good jobs' has been almost universal across the political spectrum. Yet it is not just because of Brexit and the Covid-19 pandemic that the UK – and much of the Global North – has suddenly discovered a labour shortage, although they are contributing factors.

Populations are ageing fast. Birth rates are falling off a cliff. Britain is just one of many nations where the number of children born per woman – 1.6[2]– is well below the replacement level (2.1). The population debate is turning around 180 degrees. Sometimes frighteningly so, with populists wanting to turn women into baby machines, to adopt dictatorial pronatalist policies extending even to anti-abortion and anti-contraception moves. But we know – from the children stunted and damaged by malnutrition and obesity, to the people trapped, depressed, in 'bullshit jobs' (as so powerfully defined by the late, great David Graeber, philosopher of the Occupy Movement), to those whose health has been blighted by poor housing or filthy air and water – that vast amounts of human potential is destroyed, damaged, prevented from flowering by our current systems. We cannot afford to allow that waste to continue.

The growing UBI movement

Even in 2012, when I was elected leader of the Green Party, I spoke a lot about universal basic income at public meetings, but we did not put it into the mainstream media on the very few occasions we got access to it. It was just too far outside the Overton window.

Thankfully that has changed. There has been a lot of work by academics, notable among them in the UK being Louise Haagh, Guy Standing and Simon Duffy. In global politics, Andrew Yang in the United States and Lula da Silva in Brazil (whose Bolsa Família was a conditional payment, but did a lot to spread the idea of cash payments for the poor) have raised its profile. Even tech billionaires, from Elon Musk to Silicon Valley's Sam Altman (if on the unproven premise that their technology would replace human labour) are spreading the idea of UBI. But most crucially of all, movements backing UBI have spread. I know most about the Universal Basic Income Lab Network, now with local activist groups widely distributed across the UK and beyond, as well as interest-based groups – disability, arts, women, LGBTQIA+ and more. But there are many more similar UBI campaign groups around the globe.

The idea of trialling UBI has spread fast. On one level, that focus on trials is a bad idea. To repeat the words of an Indian academic I heard speaking at a global UBI conference: 'We did not trial the end of slavery.' If a trial runs for two, or even five or ten years, recipients know it is going to end, so it is not a real UBI. And they are just individuals, while all around them is a society without the benefits of universal income. By definition, to really implement UBI, it has to be lifelong and societal. But, nonetheless, calling for trials is a powerful tool for spreading the word, and demonstrating in particular the public health benefits, as one of the most famous examples, in Finland, did very clearly. 'The basic income recipients were more satisfied with their lives and experienced less mental strain than the control group,' researchers at the University of Helsinki concluded.[3]

If we look back to the rise of Thatcher and Reagan and their neoliberalism, that did not pop out of nowhere. There had been decades of academic work, of campaigning, of think-tanks grinding away, developing arguments before the moment the monster was hatched. The work over decades, the work stepping up now, is the foundation on which a basic-income society will be built.

Purely a foundation

Universal basic income, it is crucial to say, is not a panacea. Nothing solves every problem, and anyone who tells you they have found one simple policy to transform the world should immediately be dismissed from serious consideration. But it is an essential foundation of freedom and choice – people deciding how to use their talents, time, energy and skills for themselves vastly lifts the possibilities for solving our economic, social, environmental, economic and educational crises, of building the new systems for the future. That is talent, time, energy and skills we urgently need to use well, not badly, as it is used when the boss and the state makes the decisions.

Chapter 2
Education For All, For Free, For Life

The amount of information available to us is growing at an explosive rate, but we still understand little of how our physical and social worlds operate, plus we are frighteningly short on wisdom. To live sustainably and well in the world demands free, fully accessible lifelong opportunities to learn, to discover, explore and synthesise, to truly understand, and to share the fruits of that labour with others.

A world rich in knowledge demands understanding

There is a common, and deeply dangerous, fallacy that there is 'too much information'. Duran Duran used it in 1993 as the title of a song, although when you look into the lyrics, focusing on jingles for white teeth and bright trainers, it is obvious the problem is a bombardment of advertising. And let's call advertising what it is: lying for profit. This is using creative endeavour and behavioural science to try to persuade people that buying this handbag will make them successful, or that face cream more youthful. The science now tells us that a (free) walk in the woods will have far

greater positive effects, but you very, very rarely see an adver-
tisement for that.

Yet there has been a massive explosion in the volume of
genuine knowledge – in science, in social science, history,
psychology and many other fields. The eighteenth-century
encyclopaedists who sought to capture all human knowledge
in their publications were swamped, even back then. The
volume of academic publications has been doubling every 17
years.[1] China, after the great intellectual destruction of the
Cultural Revolution, is turning into an intellectual power-
house, as I found a few years ago when I did a literature
review on soil carbon for Green MEP Molly Scott Cato;
some of the most innovative papers came from there. The
Global South is getting connected – able to access information and collate it through readily accessible technology – and
share it with the world.

If we think of information as a ball, it is expanding fast in
all directions at great speed. Considering the geometry of the
information explosion, it is clear there is more and more
space between each strand of detailed knowledge, each individual PhD researcher or craftsperson plugging away at the
years of work that will eventually produce understanding of
a species, or the method of creation of a perfect object. But
saying they are deep in the detail is not a criticism. When I
finished my first undergraduate degree, in agricultural science, I used to say that I had chosen not to follow the
academic path because I did not want to spend my life
becoming an expert in the blue-winged, pink-spotted fly,
and be unable to talk about anything else. I do not regret that
decision for myself, but we also need experts – many, many
more than we have now – in that kind of detailed, specialist

knowledge. But we also need vastly more people focused on making sense of the whole, joining the few now working in fields such as Earth system science and social system theory.

Marine biology is a glamorous field, yet Helen Scales notes in her must-read *The Brilliant Abyss* that there are only 500 specialist deep sea biologists for this 65 per cent of the Earth's surface, meaning each has 2 million cubic kilometres of water to cover for an environment of which we have only the faintest of understandings. The beginnings of that knowledge can be dated back to just 1977, when the profusion of life around ocean-floor hydrothermal vents – the possible location of origins of life on Earth, where existence is built around chemosynthesis rather than photosynthesis – was discovered. Scientists collecting organisms from these depths uncover species that we struggle to find a place for on the tree of life, and whose mode of existence we have not even begun to grasp.* The human race is already causing massive damage to this environment, with deep-sea trawling, and could now be about to destroy much of the rest with deep-sea mining, without ever coming to even a basic understanding of what is there. Lots of people are fascinated by it; very few now have the chance to devote their time to pursuing that fascination. (Such sexy scientific fields typically demand years of unpaid labour and volunteering to gain access; they are overwhelmingly dominated by people able to access the bank of mum and dad.)[2]

---

* The *Xenoturbella* – a worm-like species whose nature is often described as 'enigmatic'– is well worth looking up for curiosity value.

Knowledge murdered and destroyed

Yet conversely, at a scale I cannot even begin to quantify – I do not think anyone has – we are losing both information and wisdom. Gaping holes are being gouged into that fast-expanding globe of knowledge. We are heading towards 600 languages lost around the Earth, around 10 per cent of the total now in existence, and one third of the world's languages are at risk, each with fewer than 1,000 speakers. Eighty-five per cent are yet to be documented.[3] Languages are not just collections of words, but ways of relating to and understanding the world, and the foundation of a unique human culture.

There is much more being lost even in languages that are hanging on. 'Native science' has been described by the Tewa scholar Gregory Cajete as 'a wide range of tribal processes of perceiving, thinking, acting, and "coming to know" that have evolved through human experience with the natural world'.[4] (His people developed their culture in what is now the US state of New Mexico.) We are just barely beginning to understand the ways in which peoples as geographically far-flung as the Australian Aborigines and the dAXunhyuu (Eyak) of Alaska managed land and seascapes as healthy, productive ecosystems; not the smash-and-destroy approach of industrial farming, but light-touch agroecology long before that term was invented. Recovering that knowledge, where that remains possible, or recreating it where it is not, is a project of truly monumental scale that should be applied to much of the land surface of this planet.

Traditional cultural practices, many threatened by the

homogenisation of global culture, contain deep wisdom. The Tamil women's practice of making a *kolam* – a rice-flour pattern painted before dawn on a house, business or temple threshold, as documented by the University of San Francisco scholar Vijaya Nagarajan – incorporates ecological and mathematical understanding in a lifelong action of deep caring. On a New Books Network podcast, Nagarajan speaks about uncovering a single third-century footnote that helped her understand the origins of the tradition: that to build a house you made thousands of other animals homeless. That creates an obligation to give something back to them in perpetuity. That plastic versions of these kolam are now in widespread use is a powerful demonstration of knowledge and wisdom degraded and lost – of the deeply distorted modern ideas of 'common sense'.

Many sources, many points of access

Expertise does not have to be academic or historically rooted, however. Given time – as all could potentially have in a universal-basic-income society – knowledge can be generated by simple human curiosity, or practical need. One of the most formidable scholars I have ever met was a retired china-clay miner from Cornwall, who had made himself an expert on liverworts. (I will save you looking them up: they are often described as looking like a flattened moss, and there are about 9,000 species worldwide.) He was based in a village threatened by a new incinerator. Liverworts being affected by its polluting fumes were crucial to the ecological arguments in a fight that sadly was unsuccessful, but I hope that self-taught scholar still has some of these amazing species to study near his home. There is one thread of know-ledge thickened and deepened in that exploding globe.

More good news: every data point on that fast-exploding globe of information is now more accessible than ever before. That is something the current system has delivered for us. I am just old enough to remember the age before computer databases, when I used to jangle my way around the University of Sydney library with plastic sacks of five-cent coins for the photocopy machines, voraciously seeking to capture the knowledge only available at one physical point, and in limited opening hours. I was at the University of New England (Australia) by the time computerised journal databases became available. I remember the moment when I understood their potential vividly: I was writing about warrior women in imperial Chinese history, and through the power of a keyword search, learnt that women had been playing polo in early modern China, a fact documented on the walls of a tomb I was later lucky enough to visit. The article was in a journal about the history of sport, something I would never have come across in the paper-based age.

Open access – why not everything?

Far too often, however, access to such digital material is still tied to institutional affiliation: I once travelled to Aberystwyth on a very slow train solely for a Library of Wales readers' ticket to get free access to the online academic database JSTOR. But that restriction on the growth of knowledge is slowly being removed, with open-access journals gaining more ground – and more books published under the same conditions. As I write, I have just discovered the excellent *Environmental Humanities* journal. I included on my summer reading list for Parliament's *The House* magazine, in 2021 Thomas Pradeu's *Philosophy of Immunology*, not just for its revolutionary reshaping of thinking about the very nature of biology, but also because the freely available nature of this series deserves active promotion, to encourage others to take the same path. Knowledge is now freer than ever before.

Progress has been made also by academics using alternative media to get their work out to wider audiences. I have long been a fan of the pioneering paleoanthropology blogger John Hawks, and am astonished it took me so long to discover academic podcasting, which makes knowledge available in a form accessible even while performing essential daily tasks. On Instagram, on Twitter, even TED Talks, academics are now far more part of the public sphere than ever before, even if there is a long way to go in such activities getting sufficient credit in providing opportunities for professional advancement.

Amid the horror and suffering of the Covid-19 pandemic, and the subsequent change of much of academic life to online formats, many institutions and scholars – at least the more progressive ones – have seen the opportunity to open access for all to the seminars and workshops usually held within the tight bounds of expensive tuition fees and working-hours activities. During the pandemic I got to join the Culinary Historians of Ann Arbor in a session on suffragette cookbooks,* and enjoyed many happy hours with

---

* These were used by suffragettes and suffragists as a campaigning tool, both for fundraising and to take on opponents' claims that their members were neglecting their household responsibilities.

seminars of the Institute of Historical Research, something that I'd often attended before politics took over my life. The food-history seminar is notable in its embrace of this exciting new world, its calls for papers now extended globally, without need for travel.

Where, and when, to start?

Inadequately understood information, far too little education, knowledge and wisdom compared with what our societies need, and could generate, is the context in which I turn to consider the education system. My case study is that of the UK, but there is little difference in approach in most Anglophone countries. (The Scandinavians, as in much else, take a considerably healthier approach.)

Formal schooling starts way too early – at age four or five. Children are forced to sit down quietly for long periods in orderly rows, grasp a pencil and form letters and words long before many are ready. Neoliberal 'common sense' treats children as a set of near-identical empty vessels – and the more time there is to pour 'learning' into them, the more they will hold. Energy, spirit and will are tamed just as they are developing. Children must be contained and constrained, directed by others, or else they are sent for medical or psychological treatment. As the emerging, exciting field of critical neurodiversity studies is increasingly uncovering, the range of human possibility is broad, and forcing individuals into narrow behavioural norms deeply damaging. I often think of the account of the young primary pupil expelled from a school because he could not stop tapping his pencil on his desk. A new school put a sound-deadening pad on his pencil: problem solved.

The far too early start to formal schooling has two major costs. First, many pupils are labelled as 'failures' or 'problems' just as their development as human beings is beginning. It is a label that for many will end in poverty, or prison. Secondly, those children are robbed of the creative, productive learning opportunities that come through play, socialising freely with their peers and others, interacting with the natural world – touching, feeling, tasting it – and using their energy and curiosity according to their interests and stage of development.

The average classroom now – for all that it has a fancy whiteboard – would be essentially entirely familiar to a Victorian schoolmaster. An exam is still an exam – and even bringing in the right to type rather than use an unfamiliar pen to scrawl answers would not change its nature: it is testing if you can perform according to institutional dictates within a framework that in no way reflects real life or its challenges. We continue to force pupils through the system according to age, despite the blatant injustices that creates for the youngest pupils in each class and those developing at different rates in different areas.

Education for exams, not for life

In the UK, and across much of the world, we rank children relentlessly through their school years, according to a narrow set of criteria – largely how well they do in tests and exams. Competition is at the centre of schooling; co-operation, sometimes, a suggested add-on. Door-knocking in Sheffield in 2017, I came across a father of a ten-year-old who embraced with glee my presentation of the Green Party policy of abolishing SATs (standard assessment tests, which English children take at ages seven and eleven), restoring coursework in A levels and abolishing Ofsted (the body that inspects schools). He told me with anger about how his daughter had dissolved into floods of tears in the face of the stress of SATs tests. Young people face GCSE and A-level exams (aged about sixteen and eighteen) with a message that the success of all of their lives depends on a few hours of frantic scribbling in an echoing, impersonal exam hall. It is a far from insignificant factor in our epidemic of mental ill health. Discussing this chapter, a friend in his twenties told me how he still vividly remembered being told 'If you do not get at least a C in English and maths, you will never get a job.' He now has a very good job with the Green Party, as well as being a talented musician, and I have no doubt he will go far.

Some people thrive in exams and can use them as handy shortcuts to avoid actual learning. I did for many years. I got high marks in many subjects of which I innately knew little, working out what was likely to be in the exam, cramming it into my head, then gleefully throwing away that entire mental store afterwards. I could, for about the three hours I needed to, diagram out the detail of the two photosynthetic pathways. (How did I do it? Stick the diagrams on the back of the loo door. It is infallible, for women anyway.)

Exams test how well a student does exams. They might be necessary to establish a safety-critical baseline of knowledge for engineers or doctors, but not in most roles in life. And they teach the practice of cramming, one it took me years to unlearn and return to genuine building of knowledge.

Particularly in the age of Google, memorising and regurgitating a set of agreed facts is useless, even if you do remember them. One of the saddest things I ever heard was from a teacher who said that, with great reluctance, he discouraged his 'top' students from reading around the subject, and was careful to teach them nothing outside the syllabus. To get an A-star (the top A-level mark in the UK, introduced in 2010 to further rank students, since 'too many were getting As'), everything they put on the exam paper had to be in the marking scheme. There is no freedom to learn in such a system; to 'get ahead' you cannot follow your interests or truly develop your understanding – that is 'wasting time'.

Children as economic products

In what was once 'free time', outside school hours, children whose parents can afford it are increasingly forced into classes, groups, clubs; activities designed to help them compete against their peers in the future. This is a competition in which those at the top of the financial heap are at an enormous advantage – paying for the violin lessons, the drama club, access to sporting facilities, and tutors for cramming in more of the school materials – while a free childhood, one where children roam, discover and explore for themselves, is far more equal. Yet safety fears – from traffic, from peers, from strangers – deny this to many.

Such inequality of opportunity, as well as the inequality of schools, results in deeply unequal results, a ranking of the young in our society that is far more a measure of privilege than talent or skill. The intake of Oxbridge is overwhelmingly weighted to the benefit of those who went to fee-paying schools (weirdly called 'public' schools in the British parlance, even though they're anything but, despite enjoying the status of charities). The really public schools – those attended by 93 per cent of students – are also deeply unequal, with those concentrated in the wealthier areas benefitting from parental resources and support, generally with more stable staffing, those jobs more sought-after.

Schools in poorer areas are expected to magically transform their children's lives, even though they are only in the institution for thirty hours or so a week. Teachers are told they are failing when they cannot make up for the damage done by the lack of space and quiet at home to study, inability to access increasingly crucial technology, stressed-out or ill parents, or simple hunger. No child learns well on an empty stomach. Inequality and poverty continuing through generations are perpetuated by the economic and social systems; inequality in the quality of education and other support in schools is just an additional cause of the radical levels of inequality in our societies, not a foundation. But that means we are impoverishing our own societies, robbing them of much potential knowledge, information and skill.

Systems, not silos

The phrase 'knowledge is power' is often attributed to Francis Bacon. The origins in the mouth of a man crucial to both the advance of reductive science and extractive colonialism is telling. As is, at least on one account, the cause of his death: pneumonia contracted while studying the freezing of meat.

Systems thinking, seeing the whole picture, seems to have been lacking in an old man chasing a scientific and commercial goal without thought of consequence.

For systems thinking, considering problems holistically, ranging freely in thought across disciplines and ideas, rather than breaking them down into little pieces contained in silos that apparently can be manipulated like the dials on a machine, is something that has been severely lacking in dominant intellectual traditions since Bacon. Proponents of genetic modification as a technology for agriculture are a perfect case study for the dangers of such reductionist thought. 'Tackle the impact of drought with a single gene change and cure world hunger,' they suggest. They do not acknowledge the potentially widespread impacts of changing the metabolism of plants, or that 36 per cent of the world's crop calories are fed to animals, to produce a tiny fraction of that as meat and dairy products.[5] Nor do they choose to know that nearly a billion people regularly go hungry not because of a shortage of food, but the failure to distribute it according to need. They have already done enormous damage with the Roundup Resistant© gene, inserted into soybeans, cotton, maize and many other crops, which, entirely predictably for anyone with a modicum of ecological knowledge, has led to the widespread development of 'superweeds', equally resistant to the herbicide. The Earth has been drenched with a persistent product whose disastrous impacts we are only just beginning to understand.

Every subject should be underpinned by systems thinking, yet in many visits to universities around the UK I have seen scant evidence of significant movement to end the great siloisation of knowledge. A handful of institutions spring to mind that are taking a systems approach – the Institute for Global Sustainable Development at the University of War-wick; in Sheffield, the Institute for Sustainable Food and the Grantham Centre for Sustainable Futures, which supports its students to engage in activism with their research; and the Global Systems Institute at the University of Exeter. These are the homes of today's holders of common sense – the crea-tors of new Green models of life. Pioneering this outside the university system, Schumacher College in Devon has been a leader, as has the Oxford Real Farming Conference.

Instead, universities are, more and more, pushed to work on the 'employability' of their students. They spend much time training them in interview techniques, jumping through hoops to fit within the profoundly unsustainable systems of today, rather than to be critical, creative, lifelong learners ready for a fast-changing world. I have found in conducting job interviews with the Green Party that recent graduates are increasingly difficult to separate, to really get to know and understand at interview. They have all got identikit answers to questions like 'What's your weakness?' and produce exam-technique, smooth-patterned answers to more creative questions. They're not apparently free individuals, but cookie-cut 'job-ready' products.

Education for democracy

At first glance, it seems counterintuitive that our education structures should be directed to producing limited, inad-equate knowledge. That clearly holds the great god of 'the economy' back. But it also cements and holds in place the status quo of our economic, social and political systems. I saw this pattern clearly in action when I lived in Thailand in the 1990s. Despite strong economic pressures to increase education levels to improve the capacity of the workforce, the government was extremely resistant to putting resources into the task. I saw in Isan, the north-east, the poorest part of the country, primary schools that had been told to keep pupils for a further three years of secondary education without additional resources or staff. Teachers with limited education themselves were reading the textbook one week and teaching it the next, in extended school days forced by the failure to build extra classrooms. It was not that the government did not have resources, but it did not really want an educated populace.

It is unsurprising that there is continuing resistance at all levels to a 'right to know'. The controversial US legal scholar Cass Sunstein wrote a book titled *Too Much Information*, published by MIT Press, suggesting that 'ordinary people' would be better off if there were less information on warning labels and ingredient labels, because it just confuses the poor dears. 'Free choice' has to be limited by ignorance. In the US, far-right forces want an ill-educated, easily manipulated populace, and do their darnedest to ensure minimum support for education, particularly in poor areas. Combined with the failure to invest in infrastructure, it is likely that the nation will go down in history as the first to consciously underdevelop itself, at great economic cost but to the benefit of far-right political forces. In the UK, the trend is most evident in the arts and humanities – critical thinking, examining the state of our society, our past present and future, either creatively or analytically, are not, the government tells us, 'economically useful'. Instead they want to focus on STEM (science, technology, engineering and maths), but mostly in applied rather than higher levels.

And knowledge contained in silos can only be directed towards limited ends, ends operating within the current systems. We are seeing a trend towards dumbing down, particularly of critical thinking; the ending even in tertiary education of teaching that will help understanding, particularly of the functioning of economic and political systems, right across the Anglophone world. I declare an interest in that I know some of the people affected by the gutting of the archaeology department at the University of Sheffield, responsible for innovative landscape studies that influences thinking about modern agriculture and ecological impacts. We have also seen the sacking of a swathe of critical business scholars from the University of Leicester, and the fast disappearance of many smaller speciality fields, such as Byzantine history, and multiple languages, as well as the slashing of UK government funding for creative subjects including theatre and dance (despite the huge place of creative industries in the UK economy). Even the most basic foundational biological science, taxonomy, is suffering from a massive undersupply of students and specialists – no jobs, you see, even if the circularity of that argument is obvious.

If we think of that giant exploding ball of human knowledge, what we need is both people following threads of detail deep into its heart, but also scholars, practical workers and community members skipping lightly across its surface, making connections, seeing patterns, understanding where one thread is knotted and choking another, pointing out where gaping holes are opening up. An example of where such thinking can take us can be found in *Coral Empire,* by Ann Elias. It demonstrates that the foundations of our knowledge of something much physically easier to explore than the ocean depths – the shallow, mostly continental and island-shelf shallow seas – are twisted by the falsification and colonial exploitation and racism of its early years. We need to go back and untangle the darkness – and that is undoubtedly true of every area of scholarly and practical pursuit: take a brilliant study of Portland stone, the building material of empire and class repression (from Buckingham Palace to the British Museum) and one much celebrated in the tourist brochures of today, without accompanying critical thinking about the way its extraction robbed land from local people and its ideology was linked to imperialist racism.[6]

Lost crafts

We have also lost a massive amount of practical knowledge of making in the industrial age, and failed to develop the skills for a new age. The ability to repair, to craft used objects into useful and beautiful things, to see the natural environment and understand how to work with what is there to meet human needs, rather than whack a large bulldozer over it, flatten it and start again, has almost been lost in the standardisation of construction and industrial production. A source of future wisdom and knowledge lies surely in the Green alternative of repair cafés – local places where people gather to fix things and get them back into use, certainly, but also to learn from each other and build skills. We have started to see renewed interest in what were, traditionally, women's crafts, like knitting, crocheting and sewing, for practical but also political purposes: trees in the city of Sheffield were 'protected' during the struggle against the city's attempts to destroy them by wonderful creative works that celebrated their value.

Schools, colleges and universities are now profoundly unsuited to developing the new systems we need. The model of the university of 2024, converted from a community of scholars to a business turning out corporate slaves (tethered into the system by one more privatisation – the transferring of the cost of their learning from society to the individual through student fees – built on foundations of the insecure golden goose of overseas students),[7] is clearly (and rightly) doomed. There is no reformist way forward. What is needed is a total rethink of the nature of education: its delivery, its funding, its very foundations.

Rather than a few of us, we all need to be able to access education for all of our lives. In a fast-ageing world, taking up a new passion, a new interest, career or hobby has to be a lifelong experience. You could call it freedom to think, or freedom to learn – but that is a freedom that has to be founded on time, as well as access to resources and teachers. It cannot deliver anything like what is needed if it loads those who want to learn with debt.

The Green alternative

Starting with the youngest children, rather than trying to shove them into a set of neatly sitting, exam-delivering, identikit, obedient workers-to-be (the purpose for which compulsory education was introduced), we need to allow possibilities, interests, abilities to flower, develop at their own pace. There are strong arguments for children spending some of their time with their own age group to organically develop interpersonal skills (the damage done to hothoused 'genius' scholars rushed through their education is well documented), but that does not mean that academic knowledge and practical skills have to be taught according to age.

Free education for life, available to all, needs to be a foundation of our Green future. And with a universal basic income, people can follow their interests, develop their skills and knowledge at their own pace. But of course it is only fair that the labour of producing new understanding, or drafting new ways of engaging with the world, be rewarded.

It is hard to see how that fits within anything like the rigidity of our current institutions. Rather, I see what has been developing for a quarter of a century: informal, supportive communities of people with like interests getting together. The New School of the Anthropocene is an example of the developing efforts to find alternatives.

The University of the Third Age is a longer-running example. Teach-ins regularly conducted by striking university and college staff – available to all who are interested – is another. Groundswell, the annual gathering of the regenerative agriculture community, demonstrates how such structures can be built from – literally – the soil up. I can take this back to the mid-1990s, when I belonged to an email list of copyeditors from all around the world. Members shared their grammatical conundrums, their linguistic frustrations, their life experiences and employment challenges with their peers. Occasionally we would get together when a few members were in the same city – I remember joint copyediting the menu of a 'traditional British' restaurant with predictable severity, and the amusement of a US colleague at the dish 'spotted dick' – a community of craftspeople together.

Such communities provide a significant amount of the institutional support we see now in structures such as universities and colleges. But not funding. That requires a broader reach into communities. And already we see interested readers/listeners/admirers getting together to support a scholar whose work they want to encourage. Crowdfunding – the wisdom of crowds – is used to encourage and support the best thinking, the finest productions, truly valuable products like healthy food, durable, beautiful, practical clothing or wonderful music. Cellist/composer/singer/songwriter Caroline Lavelle is one who was pushed on to Patreon by the Covid pandemic, and now extols its virtues not just as a way of funding creation but co-creating it with the input of many.

Crowdfunding – as with this book

I have become enmeshed in the universe of history podcasts, with which I have spent hundreds of happy hours (and even in a minor way contributed; I will get back to the History of the Women of England one day). Many history-podcast proponents, and many others across the enormous spectrum of podcast subjects, rely on crowdfunding, enabled to give up 'the day job' to spend their time with their passion. Patreon already funds a significant amount of scholarship and outreach: it is the ultimate in democratic, needs-based allocation of tenure, available to all. *I Know Dino*, which brings the latest peer-reviewed research on, you guessed it, dinosaurs, is another great example.

But a lot of research and work will still need significant funding, likely beyond the scale of such endeavours. Deep-sea exploration, for example, requires technology at a level unlikely to be achieved by crowdfunding. But we do not want prospective deep-sea miners, with their deep conflicts of interest, controlling it. We need to end the current dominance of business interests in funding research and scholarship; to take health research out of the hands of drug companies; farming and agronomy research from the seed, chemical and fertiliser multinationals; and research into new industrial practices and materials science from the status quo firms that have little interest in change. (Consider the long-delayed development of electric cars, suppressed by those with interests in existing production lines.) Taxing those companies – reflecting the damage they do now – and putting the money into funds whose direction is decided by direct, deliberative democracy would be a positive way forward, avoiding the entrenched interests of our current system.

There is a growing global movement particularly in health-care to get patients, and others affected, to make decisions about the direction of funding and research questions. In 2000, the People's Health Assembly looked at the future of primary care; the Horizon Europe programme has been a leader in citizen engagement in deciding priorities. UK Research and Innovation supports the Sciencewise pro-gramme. But a lot more could and should be done, not just in hearing from the public, but acting on their views.

Chapter 3
DIY Politics

In the Green alternative future, politics is local, decentralised and often deliberative. Parliament reflects the views of the people. It is not trapped in a Victorian 'Great Man' paradigm.

Back in 2018 the University of Sheffield politics department asked me to be the discussant at a lecture given by American political philosopher Jason Brennan, author of *Against Democracy*. I was polite. I did not explicitly call the book arrogant, ill-informed and incredibly Anglo-centric. But there was, in academic terms, blood on the floor of the small but packed subterranean lecture hall by the time the discussion had finished. Brennan dismisses voters as ignorant and irrational, suggests the late-twentieth and early-twenty-first centuries 'prove' that democracy does not work, and goes on to propose a form of 'meritocracy' in which – surprise, surprise – people like him, educated and rich, get to make decisions for the rest. His case studies are mostly North American, and occasionally British. I pointed out that before dismissing democracy wholesale, the US and UK might like to try it. For Brennan did not look to the Scandinavian countries, New Zealand, Germany, indeed the majority of the world generally described as democratic, where modern voting systems and functional constitutions provide a quality of governance, and a level of democratic engagement, that make the UK and US look like the archaic oligarchic systems that they are.

Breakdown does not just happen 'somewhere else'

I said in Sheffield – explicitly – that expressing anti-democratic sentiments was dangerous. That was driven home in 2021 by the so-called Washington 'Capitol Riot', and subsequent studies that show more than 20 million Americans would back a violent overthrow of their system to restore Donald Trump to the White House.[1] Later in 2021, I listened to exiled Turkish activist Ece Temelkuran, author of *How to Lose a Country: The Seven Steps from Democracy to Dictatorship*, crystallise from the outside the arrogance of the US, the UK, France and other Global North nations who think that the collapse of political systems happens elsewhere, failing to grasp that their own are tottering and terribly, frighteningly, fragile. 'It could happen to you too,' she said.

Donald Trump is on record as saying that should he win the next presidential election: he intends to keep power indefinitely. Boris Johnson went with extreme reluctance and foot-dragging. The old rules – relying on 'good chaps' to do the right thing when their time is over – no longer work (in as much as they ever did).*

---

* The 'good chaps' theory of government is a phrase coined by constitutional historian Peter Hennessy for a perceived shared understanding of good behaviour in political life, and trust that individuals will abide by

The UK is not a democracy

I have no doubt Brennan was clear on what I thought of his work. He was seated beside me at the subsequent dinner, and never turned in my direction. I enjoyed a great discussion, however, with some of the academics who invited me. Perhaps they had predicted how I would react to Brennan's book. Over my first couple of years as Green Party leader, from 2012, I'd been touring the country saying 'we need to reform our democracy'. Then one day it struck me that describing the UK as a democracy was a profound mislabelling. When, as happened in 2019, Boris Johnson can win 44 per cent of the votes in the general election, representing the support of about 37 per cent of registered voters, then take 100 per cent of the power in the House of Commons, that is not democracy. When the Greens and UKIP combined can win 16.4 per cent of the vote in 2015 – the 1.1 million votes we collected were more than we had won in every previous general election added together – yet still remain in exactly the same parliamentary position as before – one and nought seats respectively – that is not democracy. When Parliament does not reflect the views of the people – when whole counties can be represented by a single party, based on around 40 per cent of the vote, the people unable to see any other representation in whatever direction they look – that is not democracy.

So one day – sadly I can no longer remember the venue – I

that understanding, which he says is at the heart of the UK's uncodified constitution.

took a deep breath and said, 'The UK is not a democracy.' I expected a strong audience reaction. Instead, I got a couple of moments of pause, facial expressions of contemplation, then a slow wave of thoughtfully nodding heads. That is a reaction I have seen hundreds of times since, and it is something I say in almost every talk I give, including to the Sefton Park Women's Institute, one of the locations where I was particularly unsure of the response. Although I am not sure if the statement has ever registered with the right-wing *Express* newspaper, which responded with a small explosion of indignation when I said on LBC radio in 2016 that the EU was more democratic than the UK, for at least the makeup of the European Parliament reflects the views of voters. The one strong reaction I have had was from a sixth-form economics student who pointed to a table in *The Economist* naming the UK and US as among the world's most democratic states. I responded by reflecting on the problem of 'garbage in, garbage out' when it comes to statistics.

'Take back control' was a perfectly reasonable demand

In the last democratic elections conducted across the UK, for the European Parliament in 2019, the Green Party got 11 per cent of the vote. That is a reflection of the base level of support we get – with almost no media coverage – and in a democratic system would be a solid base to build from. But it is not for the Green Party's sake that I call for proportional representation in the UK. It is for the sake of making the

United Kingdom a democracy, and tackling the deep discontent at our political framework.

For the first-past-the-post electoral system was the key factor in the result of the Brexit referendum in 2016. The winning slogan – one repeated to commentators across the land by voters (including many who had previously been non-voters) – was 'Take back control.' And as I said at the time, that was an entirely understandable and defensible cry. It was heard particularly in Northern England and South Wales, where Labour had taken its voters for granted for decades. The party's strategy was guided by the electoral system to target swing voters in swing seats – most usually the Midlands – taking its policies, and interest, far from Northern and other communities hit so hard by the depredations of Margaret Thatcher.

All of those frustrations apply – possibly even more so, starting from a far lower base – in the United States. The same Green future I am proposing for the UK could apply there. Although that is someone else's problem, I am astonished that I hear almost nothing about attempts to reform the US constitution. It was constructed to be almost impossible to change, even to secure a women's equal rights amendment. Australia's newer constitution suffers from the same issue demonstrated in the tragedy of the Indignous Voice referendum.

Westminster in control

It was not only the electoral system that provoked the 'take back control' cry. It was also the – surprisingly little understood – fact that the UK is the most centralised polity in Western Europe. Power and resources are concentrated in Westminster, and what little control local government had a couple of decades ago has been squeezed away. Anger at the imposition of house-building targets from Westminster on communities without the schools, medical services or transport to support them stretches right across the country. That is from the leafy Surrey stockbroker belt to Sunderland, the only city in the country losing population, which still faced, one time I visited, a large development of 'executive homes' on a well-loved and heavily used patch of green belt, for residents who worked in Newcastle or Durham and would have little to do with the city.

Councils are now little more than an arm of central government – treated as agents, not decision-makers – delivering, with inadequate funding, the statutory responsibilities decided by Westminster, and blamed by residents for failing to make decisions that Westminster will not allow. Their financial position varies from collapsed (the situation of a few that more are certain to join) to desperate, with a decade of Tory decisions taking money away from the poorest areas, with most pressure on children's services and social care. First-past-the-post voting systems have made many councils – at least until recently – one-party states, the entrenching of a single source of power opening the way to corruption and nepotism.

Amazon warehouse or call centre?

Another reason for the resonance of 'take back control' is the lack of economic democracy. With the unions eviscerated by decades of repressive legislation (maintained under Labour governments as much as Conservative), workers have been left to the untender mercies of giant multinational corporations. These companies are hugely profitable. They typically stash their profits in tax havens, imposing zero-hours contracts, low wages and awful conditions that see human beings increasingly treated like robots, controlled by algorithms. Workers do not feel in control because they are not.

We get the politics they pay for

Election funding by the mega-rich and the oil and mining companies is not as dominant in the UK as in the US – in part because the trade unions remain a significant balancing factor in funding Labour – but it is still huge, and the influence of big money in politics obvious. 'He who pays the piper calls the tune' does a lot to explain the policies of the larger political parties. That is without adding in the combined effect of the neoliberal ideology of 'business knows best' with the impacts of austerity that have hollowed out numbers and expertise in government departments.

There is a revolving door between business and government, something Green MP Caroline Lucas has done a lot to highlight, perhaps most notably between the gas companies and the energy department in its various guises. Even with the best will in the world, could you really expect these short-term 'bureaucrats' – serving a year or two away from their private enterprise careers – to be able to make judgements for the common good? And what is that about PwC (formerly PricewaterhouseCoopers, a giant oligopolist financial firm) and their cronies 'donating' services to both the largest parties to develop their policies[2]?

How to get to a modern functional constitution?

In one respect at least, there is a clear division between the constitutional position of the UK and the US. The UK not only lacks a modern, functional, developed constitution, it lacks a codified one. Instead it has a centuries-long series of historical accidents slapped together over vastly changing times. I unintentionally upset the *Financial Times'* respected legal editor with a letter promoting a written constitution,[3] and had to take the sensible course of not pursuing a Twitter row. But I was aching to point out that the reason I was so keen on a written constitution – aside from the fact that producing one would have to involve a national debate on the subject – is not that a codified guide is more likely to be followed. There are plenty of case studies around the world to disprove that. Rather, writing down how things are now would expose the absurdity and gaping democratic deficits in our current arrangements. Recording that the heir to the throne (remember this is supposed to be a constitutional monarchy, in which the sovereign plays no part in politics) gets to see legislation before it is tabled, and comment – voluminously – on it, as exposed by the *Guardian* in the so-called 'black spider letters' from then Prince (now King) Charles,[4] would surely cause the ink to fly off the page in incredulity.

Also, codification would ensure everyone could easily learn how the system of government works. Having laws in a written form as an essential democratic measure has a long history – go back to Ancient Rome, when the production of the Twelve Tables, making sure all citizens could know the law and so be equal before it, was a crucial step towards a functional republic.

So the Green alternative has as one of its principal pillars a new constitution for the UK: a democratic constitution in which power and resources are held locally and only referred upwards when absolutely necessary; considerable use is made of deliberative democracy; representative decision-making bodies are genuinely representative; political parties are state-funded; big money is kept out of politics; and the rules governing this are written down for all to see and debate. And it should have a regular review process – say every fifteen years – with an expectation of change, a changing world having been built into the system. That is just common sense.

A route map

So how do we get from here – a situation where we get the politics a few pay for – to a modern, genuinely democratic system?

In the depths of the Brexit parliamentary deadlock, I was at a meeting of Make Votes Matter, a wonderful, youth-led, grassroots-based campaign group operating single-mindedly with the intention of winning a proportionally elected Commons. 'We have to be ready for a constitutional crisis,' said a Lib Dem peer who has long been involved with the Electoral Reform Society. I had to restrain myself from screaming,

'What is this?' We were then, and even more clearly now, in crisis – one that is only likely to get more critical.

The job of everyone campaigning for democracy is to ensure that when things come to a head, as they soon will, when the nation asks, 'What do we do now?', 'Give the power to the people' is the logical answer. A people's constitutional assembly – a representative group of people from around the nation of all ages, backgrounds and views – should be assembled to decide what the new constitution should look like, given time and access to experts, facilitated discussions and debate. It is an approach used with great success in Ireland on issues of equal marriage and abortion rights, and in both cases showed the people to be far more progressive, and braver, than the nation's politicians.

Unfortunately it got little attention, due to the swamping news impact of Covid, but the UK did have a Climate Assembly in 2020, which came up with sensible proposals, as did a similar French event. The French assembly, interestingly, recommended that domestic flights be banned between locations covered by train journeys of four and a half hours or less. The government chickened, however, and only applied the rule to train journeys of 150 minutes or less.

Proven model

The constitutional assembly was an idea developed by the Electoral Reform Society in a trial in autumn 2015. With limited funding and time, the society nonetheless managed to run effective trial assemblies in Southampton and Sheffield, in which, given the limitations, they chose to focus on potential reforms to local government. I attended the wrap-up meeting, where assembly members joined academics who had been assessing their work to discuss the process, which was generally agreed to have provided a proof of concept. I spoke to a typical panellist, a recently retired newsagent from Southampton. He and I might not have shared lots of political views, but it was obvious how, despite having never paid more attention to politics than a regular, dutiful vote, he had really engaged with and grappled with the issues under discussion. This truly was deliberative democracy in action.

Deliberative democracy has not been widely used – taking decision-making from politicians and giving it to the people proving less than popular with circles in power – but there is sufficient evidence to show that, properly run, it is in no way a turn towards shallow popularism. It reflects a long, deep strand of British legal thinking in the form of juries, which history has shown over centuries to be generally a very solid form of decision-making. During the Napoleonic Wars – with Britain using paper money extensively for the first time – the law was merciless. If you were found in possession of forged paper money, you would hang. But juries knew that many of the accused were illiterate, were victims of crime themselves, not criminals, having no way of knowing they held forged papers. And so the juries found them not guilty, in defiance of the letter of the law. In the modern era we have seen jury after jury acquit anti-war protesters acting against military paraphernalia, from guns to warplanes, on the principle that they were honestly acting to prevent greater harm, and in Bristol we saw the 'Colston Four' acquitted for toppling the statue of a slave-owner into the harbour.

A people's constitutional assembly could, of course, in this modern era, be part of a nationwide conversation in which everyone could take part. In the age of social media its activities would be the subject of acute national interest and debate, and that discussion would feed into the assembly's deliberations. I would hope every school, college and university in the land would engage their students in the debate, and I would hope it would spread too to workplaces and community centres.

It is just common sense to debate and settle on a modern, functional, democratic constitution by means of a national conversation. The citizens' assembly would of course write down its conclusions, providing the framework for the lawyers to put into a final form.

What form of democracy?

I have less-than-fond memories of the 2011 referendum on switching to the Alternative Vote system (as used by Australia), under which candidates are numbered by the voter in order of preference, so that it is possible for the candidates to whom the majority are strongly opposed to be eliminated. Those memories chiefly consist of standing on doorsteps, saying uncomfortably, 'Yes, it is not very good. It is not proportional representation. But it is a little better than what we have now.'

It is no wonder that referendum produced the huge defeat that it did. I regularly resort now on Twitter to the simple explanatory hashtag #AVisnotPR to explain, no, we have never had a vote on a proportional system, and there is no veracity in the claim that people were voting for the status quo. They were voting against something inadequate, and that they were told was unduly complicated.

That is why I strongly resist being drawn into debates about 'what kind of proportional representation?'. Doing that makes proportional representation sound complicated. Do you prefer Additional Member System (AMS) or Alternative Vote plus (AV+) or Single Transferable Vote (STV)? What is really complicated for voters is our current first-past-the-post system, where a huge percentage of voters have to try to guess how everyone else is voting, so they can vote for what they regard as the second-least-worst candidate, to stop the worst getting in. Whereas with proportional systems, you vote for what you want, and get it. Parliament reflects the views of the people. It is not complicated, but making it look so is an obvious tactic for fans of the status quo, and a danger proponents of change must avoid.

Elections for the Scottish Parliament and the Senedd, and for the London Assembly, are already conducted under AMS – and the Scottish councils and Northern Ireland Assembly under STV. If those electorates can cope with proportional systems, so can the rest of the country. And all of those institutions have been created, or reformed, in recent times. No one would start from scratch now with a first-past-the-post system, where something like 70 per cent of votes do not count (the 'excess' votes for candidates winning hugely having no impact, just as the majority of votes against most MPs do not).

A final thought on proportional systems: will not that let in UKIP or the Brexit Party – or worse? Well, yes, we would see explicitly far-right MPs elected. That reflects the views of a small minority of voters. But if – as is the case in most European countries – the rest of the political sphere acknowledged that such views are unacceptable and dangerous, those MPs would not get power. By contrast, in two-party first-past-the-post systems, those forces just have to grab control of one of the main parties (see Donald Trump, Boris Johnson and quite possibly in the future Suella Braverman) and they get 100 per cent of untrammelled executive power.

What about going direct to the people for every decision?

I do not hear it so much these days, but there is a strand of opinion in the UK that we could do away with councils and parliaments altogether, and simply have deliberative democracy on every subject. You would get home every evening and lodge your votes on everything from brewery regulation to prison policy. Because there is no technological limit on the number of internet votes, proponents suggest, they should be used for every decision under the sun. But there is one big problem with that theory: the level of time, interest and attention we have to spare. Even with a four-day week as standard, or a three-day week, and universal basic income, do we really want to spend the newly freed time paying careful, deliberative attention to such topics? I very much doubt it. Most would regard spending time with family, friends and community – making decisions about things that directly affect them – as time much better spent. This would not be participatory, deliberative democracy, and would be at high risk of takeover from vested interests and organised campaigns.

Power to the (local) people

In the Green future, big decisions, providing direction on the major national topics of the day, will go to people's assemblies, but day to day there are still parish and town councils, district and county councils, and Parliament (moved out from its current, inappropriate quarters to a modern, functional building in Birmingham, far closer to the centre of the country) making laws, determining regulations and generally keeping the show on the road. I say national, because the UK is made up of nations, nations that are likely soon to become independent. I do not intend to go too far down that particular constitutional debate – many books have been written on the subject – but I note that the Scottish Green Party went independent in 1990, and advocate strongly for Scottish independence, and the Welsh Greens also back independence. That decisions should be made locally, by people affected, and the principle of self-determination, means the Green stance could fall no other way, and ties in with Green support for campaigns for a Cornish Assembly and a Yorkshire Parliament.

We have seen the government talk devolution – and deliver what can only be described as a simulation of it – with the creation of regional and city-region mayors. These structures have been imposed on communities; they often make little sense and those communities have often explicitly voted to reject them. The South Yorkshire Combined Authority (formerly known as the Sheffield City Region) mayoralty is only the most extreme example. The model puts the power in the hands of one person (almost always a man; that is the nature of what this model throws up in our society), who is supposed to represent the whole of a community. There is no local co-creation of the structure, just a few local council leaders meeting with London bureaucrats.

Everyone a leader

When I was elected leader of the Green Party, I said, and have continued to say, that every member of the Green Party is a leader – showing the way to a better way, to changing the system rather than sticking within its failed bounds. The Green parties in the UK, and most other Green parties around the world, have a co-leader model. In England and Wales that was introduced because our former 'principal speaker' role (which more accurately described the constitutional position) was a cause of continued media confusion.* We do not have a single figurehead, or a political philosophy named after a person. It cannot be, because it is collectively decided.

And this is just common sense. Whoever it may be, putting all political hopes onto the thoughts, the plans, the ideas – the sheer fallible humanity – of one person is something that greatly damages our politics. As is setting up elections as though they are duels between two (or a few) individuals. If you look at the countries where 'personality'

---

* And the title produced consistent media misspelling – something that particularly bugged me as a former sub-editor. They were 'principled', but that was not their title.

plays a lesser role – like most EU states – they are generally far better governed.

The Green Party's Policies for a Sustainable Society – the guiding document for our manifestos and policy decisions – has been drawn up by continual democratic work over the decades since the party's foundation. When I was first elected as leader, interviewers kept asking, 'What new policies are you going to introduce?' I kept saying, 'Policies are democratically decided at conference' – but the media just did not get it; it was not their idea of politics. Green Party philosophy and policy thus also differ from those of other parties, being stable, not swaying in the winds of political fashion, or in response to the latest focus-group result or individual flights of fancy. That is certainly a political alternative to what is generally on offer now – and a foundation for political stability, as focus on the individual is not.[5]

Far too much of our politics has not moved on from the Victorian 'Great Man' theory of history. The focus on Prime Minister's Questions from the media – a pure carnival show – is but a symptom of this far bigger problem: the reporting of politics as though it were a football game; who 'scored' with the least-worst joke. Or – in what was surely a new low for political reporting – how an individual ate a bacon sandwich (poor Ed Miliband). Those minutiae, that show, is what 'the lobby' focuses on – who is getting closer to the source of power, who is being pushed away. Policies, the business of government, what is actually happening in Parliament, is covered, if at all, by specialist education or health journalists, who have far fewer prominent column inches, and kudos, than does the lobby. The game is what matters, not the outcomes, in this current model of politics. But it does not have to be this way.

Part B

True Prosperity

Chapter 4
Restoring the Earth

A biologically and economically homogenised world – of nature or human society – is a tasteless, dull world, but more than that, it is a terribly vulnerable one. In diversity is the security of resilience, having the characteristics ready to respond to changing conditions – crucial in our current Age of Shocks.

A few years ago, on any late spring train journey around the South and Midlands of England you would see almost endless expanses of uninterrupted yellow flowers – massive fields of rapeseed. They produced an anonymous, tasteless commodity – extracted at high temperature using solvent, bleach and deodorisers to produce a uniform product for global fast-food giants and manufacturers of ultra-processed goods. More than once, watching such a scene flash by, I have heard comments in variations of 'isn't nature wonderful'. Well, no, I have to interrupt. For those fields of endless conformity were only made possible by turning the land into a biological desert, blanketed with herbicides, fungicides, hideously toxic metaldehyde to kill snails and slugs, and other pesticides. And that is a view to be found in many parts of the world, the acreage dedicated to the crop having grown sixfold between 1975 and 2007, to form the third-most-common vegetable oil in the world.[1] Just as the varieties of tomatoes and apples, aubergine and (the most extreme case) bananas that we consume have narrowed down to a small number that work best for supermarkets, a handful of multi-national seed companies have blanketed the planet with their tiny handful of products.

We have been told that we now have a new, wonderful food world, with an unprecedented range of cuisines, flavours and products available to us – scores of types of ice cream to choose from! That is what the supermarket advertisements say. And yes, I have to admit that the culinary world of my 1970s Australian childhood was vastly improved by the introduction of Indonesian, Thai, Italian and Greek flavours and cooking techniques. Anything but boiling to a pulp or frying to leather was definitely an improvement.

Yet the level of diversity in our food supplies, the variety of our diets, the data tells us, is at an all-time low, collectively if not always individually. Globally, more than 60 per cent of human calories come from just four crops – wheat, maize, rice and soybeans.[2] That is terrible for public health, and a huge risk for food security. One wheat rust sweeping the world could cause a huge shortfall of calories. Miguel de Cervantes was probably repeating a traditional peasant saying in *Don Quixote* with 'Don't put all your eggs in one basket.' But it is common sense.

Turning farms into factories

I said you would have seen those sweeps of yellow a few years ago because they are much less common now since the banning (more or less) of neonicotinoid pesticides, subject of a huge cross-European campaign reflecting the harm they cause to bees and other pollinators. It is a story that is all too familiar: new pesticide is identified (and I say identified because many of them start out as deadly poisons with other purposes, or as waste products from industrial processes) and we are told it is this wonderful new 'cure' – no side effects, no persistence, carefully targeted: just what we need. From the beginning a few express doubts, but they're drowned out. But concerns grow while commercial interests do their utmost to squash the dissenters. Fast forward: it is banned. The insecticide DDT set the pattern for what has followed, as Rachel Carson set out in *Silent Spring* in 1962.

That approach to pest management has also been reflected in other aspects of the industrial farming that has gradually taken over the planet. Deep ploughing with giant, heavy machines. Larger and larger fields, with hedges grubbed out and ponds filled. More and more application of artificial fertiliser, particularly nitrogen produced by the massively energy-hungry Haber process, despite the fact that much of the result ends up in the air and water as damaging pollution. Animals fed – if they are lucky – on fields of rye grass monoculture pumped with artificial fertilisers – or locked in stinking, overcrowded warehouses for short lives that can only be described as hell.

The extreme inefficiency of industrial agriculture is not hard to measure. It now takes ten calories of energy in – think about all those tractor passes, for ploughing and spraying, and spraying again and again – to get one calorie of food out.[3] Historically, pre-fossil-fuel use, one calorie in produced three calories out. In the climate emergency this cannot continue, but even if it were not for that, it has given us a world that a visiting friendly alien comparing, say, the year 1900 to today, would describe as utterly trashed, impoverished. She would wonder what diseases had swept the planet.

Despite that, a lot of the world's food is still produced on small family farms, mostly in the Global South. Generally less than two hectares in size, and using few fossil fuel or chemical inputs, they produce 35 per cent of food, on United Nations Food and Agriculture Organization figures.[4] But from the Bill and Melinda Gates Foundation to the World Bank, most official development assistance to many Global South governments, industrial agriculture has been seen as the future. Most funding is being directed to taking out what is left of the diversity in our food production. That means comparable changes to what we have seen in the UK – hedgerows grubbed up (50 per cent lost since the Second World War and 60 per cent of the remainder in poor condition),[5] meadows ploughed (97 per cent lost),[6] small mixed farms folded into giant monoculture spreads. It means a massive homogenisation. It means awful fragility.

Trashing our soils and animal life

That this model is unsustainable is only a statement of common sense. Agricultural land covering the size of China and India combined has suffered 'moderate to extreme' soil erosion since the Second World War, with average rates from 10 to 100 tons of soil loss per year. That is 10 to 100 times faster than it forms.[7] And that is only talking about erosion; loss of health in complex soil ecosystems is an even bigger issue. Above ground, the collapse of insect populations has recently got lots of attention, visibly obvious in that country driving no longer results in a splattered windscreen. Pesticides, and the homogenisation of the countryside, is clearly a big part of the cause – and the loss of insects rebounds right up the food chain. You almost never now see a hedgehog squashed on a road – perversely bad news, since that means there are now few hedgehogs left; a third of the already depleted UK population is thought to have been lost since 2000.[8]

Freshwater animal populations have got less attention, but when you consider they are a measure of the health of a resource crucial to humans, they should garner much more. When I was a small child, my grandparents had a holiday house south of Sydney, in the middle of a national park. 'Yabbying', catching freshwater crayfish for the pot, with a string and a bit of old meat, was a regular pastime, but by the time I was a teenager, that had stopped. The crayfish had vanished. I do not recall much comment about it. The reaction was a collective shrug and rueful false common sense: 'That's progress.'

Extinction: one side of the Anthropocene

A mass extinction is a short period of geological time in which a high percentage of species – bacteria, fungi, plants, mammals, birds, reptiles, amphibians, fish, invertebrates – dies out. The best known is the end of the Cretaceous, when an asteroid strike saw off the non-avian dinosaurs, together with much else on Earth. We are not, yet, at that scale. We're *only*, the experts say, at somewhere between 1,000 and 10,000 times the average level over the aeons. That sounds like a vast range – but we have so little knowledge of what is there. Take a sample of healthy soil, and it is likely that 90 per cent of the species in it will not be known.

But more than that – and on a path to a potentially Cretaceous-style collapse – we're seeing the loss of the vast bulk of what was wild biomass on this planet. Humankind represents just 0.01 per cent of the living animals, but over the past few thousand years (only a tiny percentage of our species' existence), we have destroyed whole ecosystems. The Yangtze River basin, now an industrial wasteland, was once as rich as the Amazon.[9] Put humans and our livestock together and we make up 96 per cent of its mammalian bio-mass. That is taking up space once occupied by diverse wild species, and relegating those to tiny areas of refuge such as nature reserves.

Our impoverished world

British campaigner George Monbiot has done a lot to popular-ise the concept of 'shifting baseline syndrome', the understanding that we consider the natural world we saw in our youth as 'normal', when anyone alive today has only seen (except in the most remote corners) an extremely depleted planet. One of the best descriptions I have read of what is within human memory is from a village in Liguria, northern Italy:

People talk about great gatherings of toads after the rain; bats swarming so thickly around the streetlights in the vil-lage that they almost obscure them; snails emerging in their thousands on the walls of the terraces; clouds of fireflies as

bright as the sparks from the fire in the church square on
Saint Anthony's day; dozens of hares racing through the light
fields of corn in the mountains; eels as thick as your arm in
the river.[10]

There is a hamlet in the Morvan National Park in France that
I can just about imagine being like that – as it would have
been a century ago. Now I see there a handful of bats and
swifts in summer, a nice flock of fifty or so sparrows and a
gathering of perhaps 150 European greenfinches in winter, a
profusion of wild and wonderful fungi in the forest in the
autumn, from the spooky devil's fingers to giant ceps that
can feed me for several days – and far better than anything I
have seen in the UK.

People were comfortably at home in naturally rich lands,
which gave them much of what they needed. This is a description of English fenland life before the wetlands were drained:

> Three thousand wildfowl had been taken from the decoy on
> Holme Fen in one week . . . Fish tapped for food; peat dug
> for fuel; litter . . . off marsh plants for coarse hay . . . Reeds
> grew in the wetter part of the fen. After winter frosts stripped
> them of their flags, old stems of four years or more were cut
> for roofing and younger stems were mixed with litter for
> fodder . . . Coopers sought the bullrushes on the fen, their
> long round stems were dried and placed between barrel
> staves where, on contact with fewer or whatever else was
> in the barrels, the stems would swell and keep the joints
> watertight. . . . Osiers from willows on the fen were cut for
> baskets, eel traps and faggot binds; thicker branches made
> good scythe handles.[11]

The people of those fens had a good life, an independent life, and they fought, hard, to defend it, as told in James Boyce's brilliant book *Imperial Mud*. Yet the military power of the state, backing the interests of the London financiers and the expertise of Dutch engineers, drained the fens, immiserated the people, and produced the giant, dull, almost lifeless expanses of unhealthy soil we see today.

'Tidy' cities and towns

The impoverishment of the natural world is not just in the countryside. The sterilisation of our farmland is reflected in the cities, particularly in the rampant use of one herbicide, glyphosate, a broad-spectrum, persistent herbicide that has attracted increasing campaigns against it on human health grounds, but which is also, finally, starting to be questioned for its Ground Zero flattening effects on all plant life. What some call weeds, I would call wildflowers. We are starting to see – although still on a small scale – rejection of that dreadful monocrop, the lawn, usually maintained by massive applications of water, fertiliser, pesticide, and fossil fuel for mowing, and attempts to allow wildflowers to bloom. But that frequently produces complaints of 'untidiness' – just ask the Green council in Brighton and Hove. Well, I say we need a war on tidiness.

Behind this has been a cultural frame – very dominant in the second half of the twentieth century – a drive for neatness. For straight lines. For order. This was illustrated for me clearly in Sheffield, canvassing for a council election in a road of seventies bungalows. It was when the battle to save the city's street trees was raging hot – the forces of multinational contractor Amey and the Labour city council arrayed against residents backed by the Green Party. Seeing my Green rosette, one resident, who had probably moved in when the house was built, told me firmly how glad she was that most of the street trees on her block had gone. They were 'untidy'. They dropped leaves and sap, sometimes on newly washed cars. They were rests for birds that left droppings on the pavement. How much neater it looked with just lines of concrete marshalling parked cars, the resident thought. How dead, thought I.

Yet the campaign Save Sheffield Trees (#SaveSheffTrees) – a huge success after brave individuals put their bodies and their freedom on the line – eventually helped educate not just the city or country, but the world. I was delighted to see that it inspired a similar campaign in New Delhi, as well as many other places closer to home.[12] There is a growing understanding about the value not just of street trees, but of all plants in our lives. A famous study found hospital patients with a view of a tree from their window recovered faster than those looking at a brick wall.[13] Simply being trapped in a world of rigid straight lines is bad for human health.[14] We evolved for the curves, the discontinuities, the untidiness of nature. Even pot plants in the house improve health.

Humans are diverse, or dead

A diverse plant community where we live and work is essential for good human health, because it affects our microbiome. Which is where we touch on the scientific discoveries over the past couple of decades that have revolutionised our understanding of our own nature. For we are not a single species, but an assemblage (a holobiont in the jargon) made up of human tissue and something like 50,000 microbial species. Without them, we are dead. Imbalances in the gut microbiome are linked to cancers, obesity, asthma, inflammatory bowel diseases and mental illnesses. That is why the United Nations has HUMI (Healthy Urban Microbiome Initiative). The more diverse our microbial environment, the healthier we are. And a more diverse diet, a more natural world around us, produces a healthier microbiome. We are animals, our wellbeing dependent on the health of our environment: that is common sense.

It is a new understanding that means we should be looking – very hard – at that 'anti-bacterial soap' over the sink, the equally labelled cleaning spray underneath it, and wondering just what we are doing to trash ourselves and our planet. (For every other animal is also a holobiont; probably some of the worst damage neonicotinoids do to bees comes from the impact on their microbiome.) In the days of Prime Minister David Cameron there was some real UK government focus on the issue of antimicrobial resistance – diseases no longer being susceptible to drug treatment – but sadly that has been diluted. Without anti-microbial drugs, we would lose much of modern medicine – not just hip replacements and kidney transplants, but the confidence that a scratch from a rose bush will not kill you. When that surface spray says 'kills 99.9% of bacteria', that means you are opening the way for the 0.1 per cent resistance to spread – and share their genes with others. (Which they do very often not by interbreeding but by literal sharing – 'horizontal gene transfer'.) If you look at the advertisements for such sprays, they are filled with shiny, hard, straight surfaces, an apparent paradise of sterility, like a laboratory. That is the model of human life and human health presented to us. Yet we know that it is a lie, a hugely damaging lie that is terrible for human public health and that of nature.

Animals as machines

There is a historic scientific philosophy behind this approach – a belief that humans can create, straighten up the world, manage it like a factory – that animals are machines and that we can create biochemical systems more efficient than nature's. The seventeenth-century philosopher Descartes' view of animals as mere automata has been pervasive, and hugely damaging. It allowed enormous sheds of factory-farmed chickens, sentient animals living a short life (often just thirty-five days in the case of 'Franken-chickens') of misery and pain. But why, when anyone who has ever owned a dog is likely to have concluded they have a 'theory of the mind' (can try to understand what we are thinking and seek to manipulate that), has Descartes' approach, this belief, been so pervasive? Well, it has been hugely convenient to the dominant economic forces in the centuries since the philosopher died. (The way in which it has bled over into the treatment of human subjects we will get to in Chapter 12.)

Traditional farmers, pre-twentieth century, understood the soil as a living, complex system, even if they lacked the knowledge of fungi, bacteria and microscopic animals that we can identify to explain it. A 1920s Italian proverb said that artificial fertiliser was 'good for the father and bad for the son'. Soil is not just dirt. (And I should warn here that I am only scratching the surface of what I consider a wonderful, amazing subject and a fascination of mine – I did get tardigrades their first mention in Hansard in my maiden speech in the House of Lords – and as I often warn audiences, I can get very geeky about soils. But I will not do that to you here. Not much anyway.)

Fungi and plants worked together to colonise the land of this planet,[15] and that intimate, complex co-operation is central to the amazing productivity and natural wealth of our planet. Between 15 and 40 per cent of the energy that plants capture through photosynthesis is directed down through the roots, into the soil to 'farm' the ecosystems that – when healthy – extract and concentrate the other nutrients that plants need. These are natural systems developed over hundreds of millennia; systems some think we can sweep aside, destroy, replace with simplistic models of plants fed concoctions of our own devising in plastic troughs, varieties modified by a snip on the genome here, a tweaking of the DNA there. This is little removed from Victorian mad-scientist territory, to take such a complex system and believe it can be managed like a machine.

Yet why is it that this kind of science remains dominant, and the ecologists, the permaculturalists, the agroecologists and those seeking to build on indigenous, long-term successful systems of production are at the margins of public discourse, and funding?

Follow the money

Medieval peasant farmers were reluctant to grow wheat. It was a difficult crop, more prone to failure than oats, rye and barley. They liked to sow a mix of grains in their fields, so whatever the conditions and disease challenges, something was likely to produce a crop. But aristocrats wanted high-status white bread, standardised, fluffy, as the Romans had valued before them. Peasants lived largely on gruel (mixing grains and legumes) and beer. Our understanding of how this society functioned is heavily dependent on manorial records that preserved no trace of a peasant woman nipping out into the forest to pick a basket of mushrooms for dinner, flavoured with herbs and sided by fresh greens and flowers. You need to go out with an expert forager into a fairly natural area to get a sense of how the world was – and to a degree still is – filled with potential food for much of the year. But there is no money to be made from dandelion leaves pinched out for a salad, or nettles boiled up for a soup.

Today's equivalent of the aristocrat is the multinational food company or fast-food giant, which wants enormous quantities of factory-farmed inputs for its factories, to turn out plastic-wrapped, concocted blends of fats, sugar and salt, to be moreish, unfulfilling and inoffensive to any palate (for which read 'tasteless'). A financialised world demands a financialised diet. Picking an apple off a tree instead of buying a sugar bar is an act of resistance – even more so planting that tree.

Restoration

The alternative model, built on strength from diversity, is, slowly and tentatively, at terrifyingly small scales, being restored. Even to our wheat crop, dominated at scale now by a handful of varieties. At the 2022 Groundswell (field days for regenerative agriculture), I was delighted to see the race of wheat (in the jargon a 'cross-composite population' made of genetically distinct plants rather than the homogeneity of industrial production) developed on the brilliant Wakelyns Organic Agroforestry hub standing well against commercial products.

I heard Kimberley Bell, founder of the Small Food Bakery in Nottingham, speaking at Oxford Real Farming Conference with passion about working with flour produced from such a field. Every batch will be different – with the season, with the fields. But this demands a different kind of economy, of small, local, skilled artisan production. Most of the bread in the UK – and the Australia I grew up in – is manufactured in giant factories through what is known as the Chorleywood process: standardised products in, standardised products out. It is a production system for supermarkets, producing so-called bread, wrapped in plastic; ultra-processed pap. And the supermarkets are now seeking with barely modified production methods to produce expensive so-called 'sourdough' that is nothing of the sort; I have been working with the Real Bread Campaign to try to stop that.

Also, in East Anglia the brilliant Hodmedods – the name drawn from the local dialect word for hedgehogs (a reminder of another almost lost diversity) – is promoting the growing of beans and lentils. Our warming climate is helping with the lentils; the beans mostly involve rescuing what were once major crops that had been almost lost. That is restoring an alternative, local, environmentally friendly healthy protein source – such a contrast to the intensive chicken and pig production that is polluting our land, air and waters, and wasting huge quantities of what could be human food.

And there are multiple small-scale efforts I have had the pleasure of visiting that aim to produce diverse vegetables and fruits, often organically, with extremely high productivity, from healthy soil. I was hugely inspired to hear Perrine Hervé-Gruyer from La Ferme du Bec Hellouin at the Oxford Real Farming Conference a few years ago, talking about their conversion of a patch of standard Normandy arable land into a hugely productive, rich small farm that is without artificial fertilisers or pesticides. A lot of its inspiration comes from Parisian history, where in the nineteenth century a sixth of the land area was used to produce more than 100,000 tonnes of high-value vegetable crops annually.

A photo of Wakelyns from the air is telling – a rich, teeming, deep patch of green in the midst of sparse, hungry fields dedicated mostly to sugar beet, a crop whose quantity of production is acutely damaging to human health, and that strips away valuable topsoil during harvest. Agroforestry – mixing trees with crops or grasslands – is, as a broad principle, one-third more productive than taking a straight arable or grassland approach. Unsurprising really, when you consider that, as permaculture principles make clear, layering of growth will have far more possibilities than only operating in two dimensions.

Walk into the garden

We have also, in recent decades, drawn another hard, neat division. The countryside is where food is grown. Cities are where it is eaten. But one Green alternative approach – which is getting a lot of attention in this age where food security is suddenly high on the agenda – is returning to food-growing in cities: in little communal plots, in personal gardens and on balconies, on what are now pointlessly mown swards of grass monoculture.

What if growing at least a little of our own food was part of everyone's life? The practice of gardening is great for health and wellbeing – that is a common-sense understanding. Personally producing food will increase respect for it. Nothing tastes quite as good as a salad you have grown yourself. And we know that allotments are some of the richest biological environments available today – great for nature. Diversity in labour, as with all other forms of diversity, is good for us.

Chapter 5
The People's Economy

Capitalism is not working. It is treating the planet as a mine and a dumping ground, and creating miserable, insecure, unhealthy societies. A Green economy is diverse; it is localised; it operates within physical limits.

It is not just the countryside that has been homogenised. Today's way of life has been too – not just the names on the shop signs, the clothes the people are wearing, the computers and the toothpaste, but also the economic arrangements behind them. That is captured in part in the UK in the term 'clone towns', but it is also true on a global scale. One framing sees the world being split into two camps: autocratic states China and Russia lined up against 'the West'. But late-neoliberal capitalism is the economic model in those states every bit as much as in the UK or US. And the technological basis, the shape of everyday life – from mobile phones to office buildings to fast food – is essentially the same.

The world has only one economic model in operation at any kind of scale, a clearly failing model, and, broadly, one essentially identical physical way of living in it. It is only common sense to see the danger in having less economic and physical diversity in the world now than ever before in human history. The late, great Douglas Adams in his *Hitchhiker's*

Guide to the Galaxy series has a planet wiped out by a disease spread via dirty telephones, in his satire a deep truth about risk of uniformity. The brilliant novel *Station Eleven*, by Emily St John Mandel, warned of the dangers of an interconnected world, long before all but the specialists had heard of coronaviruses.

Globalisation is a term most often used by economists and their critics, but it is a reality every traveller sees in the furthest corners of least-connected communities. A British football shirt or a weird American slogan on a baseball cap in Africa or the poorer corners of Asia – that is where much of the fast fashion, worn once in the Global North and discarded, ends up, containers of secondhand clothing having long displaced local weavers and tailors. Local stores in the smallest hamlet will have Coca-Cola, the quintessential, pointless, unhealthy, destructive testament to the power of advertising. They will also have shampoos and toothpastes made by giant multinational companies (likely in small plastic sachets) and ultra-processed snacks in more plastic sacks.

The Czech dissident and later president Milan Kundera, in a world much less homogenised than today's, wrote in *The Art of the Novel*, 'Unity of mankind means: no escape for anyone anywhere.' It was back in the late 1990s, in a little grocery store in Colombo, the capital of Sri Lanka, that I found in the chiller individually wrapped slices of Kraft cheese with layers of Vegemite* – from Australia, of course – and thought, 'What the hell?' The shipping of tasteless, pointless, environmentally destructive products like that

---

* The Australian rough equivalent of Marmite.

around the world – for no defensible reason – has only multiplied exponentially since then.

Bioregional diversity

The Green alternative is that economies, in their operation and structures, are far more local, not one global whole. The French have the attractive concept of *terroir* – flavours, tastes, products, specialities specific to a locality (and not just wine) – fitting its soil, its air, its people. In Italy too, cities have local independent shops, local producers and specialities – although both nations, as in the rest of Europe, also suffer from behemouth supermarkets filled with ultra-processed pap that more disadvantaged people in society are forced to rely on. A useful Green concept here is bioregions – where local climate, geography, topography, water flows and vegetation produce different environments – into which humans can choose to fit in many different ways. Why are we building towering glass office blocks, profoundly unsuited to so many of the environments in which they are built? It defies common sense.

Localisation can also work for suburbs or parts of cities. We have seen through planning and through economic pressures many communities turned purely into dormitories – gentrification taking out not just the pubs and the community centres, but also the workshops and the small businesses that once employed local people. I saw this first hand in Somers Town, between Euston and Kings Cross stations in London. Being nearly all council or ex-council housing, it resisted gentrification, but the places where the residents once

worked, the warehouses and stores around the train termi-
nals, have been swallowed up by redevelopment, the British
Library, the 'luxury flats' of the massive Kings Cross development, the Francis Crick Institute. (And, declaration of interest,
I was chair of the community group opposing that wasteful
disaster.)

The mayor of Paris, Anne Hidalgo, has done a great deal
to popularise the fifteen-minute city, the idea that everything
you regularly need is within a comfortable walk or cycle ride
of home. There is no commuting time. Jobs far from homes
are disastrous, for health, wellbeing and the environment.
Pre-Covid, the UK had double the average commuting time
of the rest of Europe and double the rate of relationship
breakdown, two statistics surely interrelated.

Specialisation where it makes sense

I am not talking of autarky, either at the bioregional or
national level – as per North Korea or communist Albania –
where the different, the foreign, is kept out. Rather, each
community has a chance to draw in different influences, different local resources, be influenced by local preferences, to
change and flex and develop according to democratic choices.

Complex medical machines and mobile phones will
always be made in only a few places that have specialised in
the necessary supply chains. Coffee and bananas will never
(we hope) be grown in the UK, unless climate change is
allowed to really run wild. The presence of one local entre-
preneurial craftsperson, where there is a big supply of reusable
timber, might encourage a town to be a specialist in producing

fine furniture; in another hill town some keen knitters combined with surviving traditional culture might make it a centre for fine jumpers made to last a lifetime.

Trade in a Green world is not just fair trade, but only the necessary, positive trade that improves lives. A few years ago (pre-Brexit), graphs on trade in ice cream between the UK and the Continent were telling. The figures – for both imports and exports – were large, and had been growing fast. That was utterly pointless environmental waste (all those diesel-driven compressors on lorries) and wasted human labour. Sure, swap recipes! Maybe move some spices or special fruits. But not frozen ultra-processed foods.

Prosperity built on local foundations

Start with a local greengrocer, if you are lucky enough to still have one. With towns and cities surrounded by market gardens, much of her stock can come from local areas, her cash going into local economy. When she needs some new shelves, she employs a local carpenter. A new sign? A local signwriter. Sorting out the shop lease? A local solicitor. Taxes? A local accountant.

Buy goods – even if not produced locally – from such a local store, and about half of the money stays in town. Buy it from a chain store, and a couple of pence in the pound remain, the rest swooshing off, very likely to land in the nearest handy tax haven. Money that goes around and around in the community pays a local babysitter, who buys a cake with their friends in a local café, whose owner donates to a local charity.

This also means that each community has a range of people with a variety of useful skills. I cannot say as a young journalist in small country towns in Australia that covering Rotary Club meetings was my favourite task. But it was there, for all of the often annoying paternalism, that the local lawyer, accountant, shop owner, hospital manager and school head were often found, and a lot of good was done – public facilities restored, schools given extra funding, campaigns against overweening central authority organised. Transition Towns – which have done so much to develop alternative models of local prosperity – have tended to flourish in communities with at least a strong foundation of social capital. They are much harder to organise in places where almost everyone is struggling just to keep their household above water.

Build such roles out of communities and you're taking away the local social capital. And young people who want to advance have to leave their communities, usually never to return. This is a trend that is only accelerated with the growing dominance of a handful of companies and extreme competition between them. We have recently seen major supermarket chains taking the managers out of their stores, leaving a central computer system to make most of the decisions, with lowly paid local workers to implement them.* (In 2020 Morrisons cut 3,000 managers from their stores after a 'disappointing Christmas'.)

---

* I went collecting signatures with the campaign group Sheffield Needs a Pay Rise years ago on its petition calling for a £10-an-hour minimum wage. We found plenty of people with 'manager' on their nametag in chain stores happy to sign, not just for their colleagues, but themselves.

Today's model for human and environmental destruction

T-shirts sold in those very same stores, shipped, barely worn, in bales of secondhand clothing to the Global South, have often travelled truly astonishing distances. They might have started out as cotton picked in Uzbekistan by children as young as thirteen or fourteen, forced out into the fields by a dictatorial government; then shipped to a factory in China to be dyed and spun into cloth from a factory spewing its waste into a local river; then off to Bangladesh to be sewn up in a sweatshop factory under conditions that can be deadly – as the Rana Plaza collapse that killed more than 1,000 demonstrated – and are certainly exploitative. Then that T-shirt is shipped to a chain store on a UK high street, to be sold by a minimum-wage, zero-hours contract worker, the profits – and there will be big financial profits – very likely ending up in a tax haven. (See the £1.2 billion paid in 2005 by Philip Green, former chairman of the retail group Arcadia, to his wife, resident in Monaco.) Every step of the way has involved fossil-fuel transport, carbon emissions, air and water pollution, and human exploitation.

Increasingly, the garment will not be cotton, but artificial fibre – in simple terms, plastic. The volume of clothing sold in the UK now is double that of a decade ago (and I do not remember people walking around naked or in rags then). That makes us the world's second-largest secondhand clothing exporter. (The US is the number one.)[1] Seventy per cent of what goes into 'recycling' goes overseas, much of it to Ghana, and much of it is of such poor quality that it is not even any use for resale, so ends up being dumped.[2] Instant pollution. Another destination is Chile, with an estimated 39,000 tonnes dumped in the Atacama Desert.[3]

Significant volumes of clothing and shoes never even make it out of their initial wrapping. Burberry, after an outcry, vowed in 2018 to stop burning its own products to ensure they could not be sold 'too cheaply', but it just happened to be the brand that got caught. Louis Vuitton, Nike and H&M were just some of the others named for the same practice.[4] That is what happens when the externalised costs of making a product – from the child labour to the sweatshops, the use of scarce fresh water and soil destruction, the climate emissions and air pollution – are borne by all of us, and not just the maker. That the full costs should be the responsibility of the manufacturer, and the purchaser, is just common sense. The multinationals now are recipients of massive subsidies, the cost of their businesses weighing on all of us.

The planet treated as a mine and a dumping ground

Furniture, toys, seasonal decorations, electronic gadgets and tools also get discarded before, or soon after sale, ignoring the human labour and environmental cost of their manufacture. We are treating the planet as a mine and a dumping ground, for 'profit'. There is an annual UK news story, a media standard, about the arrival before Christmas in the UK of the *Ever Ace* – 'the world's largest container ship' – capable of carrying 23,992 boxes of steel, each enclosing thirty cubic metres of 'stuff'. It is 'the nation's Christmas presents', the stories say. You will see the 'stuff' arrive, in the pound stores, in the toy stores, in the supermarkets: giant, flimsy, plastic Santas, 'stocking filler' tat, plastic Christmas jumpers. Soon it will be in the landfills and incinerators, polluting our air, contaminating our waters, heating our planet.

My (adopted) father's mother was born in the first decade of the twentieth century. When Grandma was married, in a manner classic of the time, she got a set of (relatively) expensive solid wooden furniture, all still in use when they celebrated their fiftieth wedding anniversary. Grandma was, to my parents in seventies Australia, an embarrassment, a leftover from another age. She had drawers of string, rubber bands and plastic bread bags ready for reuse, wore patched clothes and made her own jam and chutney. My parents thought this was living in poverty (although the household was not poor); this was not 'modern', they considered. Now I know that it was a life full of common sense.

Sadly, as a child I was never allowed to get to know this grandma, but I am pleased that in my late teens and twenties I did. She told me a story of how a relative had lost a pair of scissors and just shrugged, intending to buy a new pair. But Grandma started a hunt and found them, rusting, in the rubbish pile, wrapped up in flower trimmings. 'I coated them in oil and sandpapered them, and here they are,' she said, pulling them with a flourish from a drawer. She was, I thought later, trying, in her modest and unassuming way (she spent those fifty years essentially as a servant to her husband – and a victim of what we would today call coercive control), to make a broader point about society's pointless waste.

The Green alternative approach acknowledges that every resource, every human hour of labour, has real value, must be cherished and acknowledged, treated with respect. The figure on the price tag of every product has to reflect its real costs, be borne by the company that made it, not carried as a huge subsidy for its profits by the rest of us. One way of approaching this would be to change value-added tax to capture those costs. A T-shirt made from hemp grown in Kent, spun into cloth in a local factory with excellent worker and environmental conditions, sewn up by a local tailor, might well be tax-free. That T-shirt starting with cotton in Azerbaijan, with the full costs included, would not be able to compete.

Choice. What choice?

But consumers want these items. They buy them. Blame the consumers. We're just catering to 'the market', companies say. Just as the right of politics tries to blame obesity on individuals' 'choice' or 'lack of willpower', so this massive, unsustainable waste is blamed on 'people'.

I have three answers for that: poverty, misery and advertising.

Being poor is expensive, and it is massively environmentally destructive. A classic example sets out the problem. You only have £10 in your pocket, but your shoes have fallen apart (and they are certainly not made to be repaired). You buy a new pair of shoes for £10. You know they will only last a few months, at best. They will be poorly made. Uncomfortable. But you need shoes. And four times in a year you will buy those shoes. Every year. The cost over ten years: £400. A rich person – say your boss – decides they need a new pair of shoes. They spend £100 on shoes that will last five years or more, that can be repaired. That are likely made of organic materials that could even be composted back into soil. They are comfortable. For five years, or more, they have those shoes. Maybe once or twice they are resoled. They are still financially far ahead.

A critic might say 'but many items sold are not as essential as shoes', and that is true. And maybe some of them are, or could be, longer-lasting, even seasonal products like a winter coat. But poor people live in smaller homes, homes that, if they have been built in the past few decades, have tiny rooms with little or no storage. And poor people – renters – have to move often, as landlords hike the rent, or reject requests to fix the heating and throw them out in a revenge eviction. We are not talking about a fancy moving company here – perhaps a mate with a small van, if you are lucky. Items are not kept from year to year, season to season. They cannot be. There is nowhere to keep them.

But what about those flimsy giant plastic Santas that fill discount stores at Christmas? No one has to buy those, do they? Well, imagine you are a parent. Your child could not go on the school trip to the theatre because you could not afford it. They want the latest games console for Christmas, although they know you are worried about money, so have not asked for it. You are feeling guilty. You know your child is missing out. They are struggling to do their homework at the kitchen table while minding their younger brother and cooking dinner because you are at work. Being poor is miserable. You want some cheer, and the giant Santa costs about the same as a bus ticket.

The Green alternative starts with universal basic income and includes a real living wage: payment for every person's labour that acknowledges their worth, gives them the funds they need. It takes away the hunger, the desperation – and gives time to consider purchases slowly, carefully. And it tackles one huge push-factor in consumption: advertising.

Advertising misery

Everywhere you look, there is advertising. There is no escape: on public transport, on the internet, on television, on billboards, even in pub loos. Advertising uses some of the most creative brains we have, to tell you that you are unhappy now, but you will be happy with this handbag, this soft drink, this label on your shoes or this car presented as swooping across the prairie, even if you will only ever drive it on a city street. Sometimes it will not obviously be advertising. Maybe that hot new influencer, or latest James Bond, is swinging a branded jacket over their shoulder, or the *Daily Mail* is telling you what dress a royal is wearing, or what boots the latest football star favours.

And you are miserable. You are stuck in a bullshit job, the rent is going up, and you are feeling guilty about that comfort-eating hamburger you grabbed on the way home. You shop.

And you are told that you *should* shop. After all, the government is worried about consumption falling. In 2022 household expenditure accounted for 63.5 per cent of GDP in the UK. By spending money on cheap and cheerful tat, or on expensive brand names, you are helping ensure that the next quarter's figures are being cheered on the evening news, rather than mourned.

The Green alternative is to clamp down on this unhealthy, stressful bombardment: there is no 'right to advertise'. We can choose what to allow, and a good place to start would be banning gambling and alcohol advertising (which is a public health disaster in promoting addiction), and that aimed at children (those under eleven lack the capacity to distinguish between advertising and editorial). And to replace the bombardment of billboards on our streets and public transport with something better – trees and flowers, and more, far more, public art. (Poems on the Underground in London is a great scheme. Why not have that in every community?)

Planned obsolescence

Even if you can, and do, buy those expensive brand names that bombard you from every quarter, there is no guarantee of longevity in the products you purchase. Apple is, it likes to claim, the perfect brand of the twenty-first century – and it is the perfect case study for our disastrously destructive economy. Overpriced, overhyped, heavily advertised products made by abused labourers far away that are actively designed to demand replacement within a few short years, or even months: common sense is that the world cannot afford Apple or its ilk.

But it is not just the 'star' products. This is the norm. A few years ago, I went on social media to grumble about my fridge dying after six or seven years. 'You were lucky it lasted that long,' was the chorus I got back. Decades ago, appliances such as washing machines, hobs and dishwashers lasted decades. And they were mostly mechanical, so if something broke, they could be repaired. Now they have all kinds of fancy electronic bells and whistles. (I know I am far from the only person who almost never uses them.) And once they go wrong, that is it.

The Green alternative starts with the Right to Repair, now a formal campaign that has been (if inadequately) written into UK and EU law. Making a product means you also must make the spare parts to repair it should something go wrong, and provide the information needed for the repairer to do the job. Many of us these days lack the skills, but we have seen a growing movement of repair cafés: human creativity and knowledge being put to good use.

The Green alternative does not just think about repair, but also disposal, when necessary, to manufacturers and sellers being responsible for their products – their real costs including that of the end of life (which sees off new nuclear power plants). There has been widespread talk for more than a decade of moving from the provision of goods to the provision of services. I visited that long ago at the National Union of Students head office, where a multinational company had provided not the light bulbs, but the lighting, with a contract to ensure the necessary lumens and thus an interest in providing as durable a product as possible. The model exists and it works. We just need the legal and institutional frameworks to make it the norm.

One of everything for every household

One reason for the failure of service contracts to take off may lie in the individualisation of much of our lives. It was not once the case, and it still is not in many parts of continental Europe, but it is assumed in the UK that even the tiniest, most improbably little flat will still have its own washing machine. Laundrettes – a neighbourhood location that would once have been a centre of sociability and support – have almost disappeared, pushed out of many areas by high rents and business rates. People with lawns (yes, those dreadful monocultures) the size of handkerchiefs have their own lawnmower – and probably hedge clippers for their tiny stretch too.

The Green alternative – sharing – can be found modelled around the country, in co-housing schemes (intentional communities of private homes with shared spaces) and Transition Towns. At Lancaster co-housing, I stood in the laundry room, with its shared washing machines and (for when really necessary) dryers. There is a communal lawnmower shared between scores of householders. (And co-housing offers an important corrective to the 'need' for more space in individual houses for entertaining. A communal big space that can be booked for that family party or teenage bash means less space needed within homes.)

It was in Frome, at its 'Library of Things', that I learnt that the average electric drill is used for fifteen minutes in its lifetime. How much simpler, cheaper and far less destructive to nip up to the library when you want to install that shelf. And if a child wants to learn the guitar, rather than buy one that will languish in the attic, if not be consigned to landfill, when enthusiasm wanes, an instrument can be borrowed. The library does not have to buy things. They are donated – more 'stuff' out of landfill – and if it does have a lot of pasta makers, well, some celebrity chef might again have a hit show using them, and they can be rolled out for the duration.*

GDP – the economists' false god

Sharing rather than buying demands more change than the creation of new forms of local libraries. Rishi Sunak is promising us growth. Sir Keir Starmer, for the opposition Labour Party, criticised the Conservative Party on its record of growth, promising to supercharge the UK's. Even chatting to a Labour peer, very much on the left of the party, with whom I agree about much, when I start saying that growth must not, cannot, be our target, I lose him. This, like the idea of jobs as the way to define people's position in society, is where Green political philosophy departs from both the right and the left.

In part, that is an environmental departure. You cannot have infinite growth on a finite planet. That is not politics, it is physics – and common sense. With the planet at or beyond its boundaries on climate, on biodiversity, on biogeochemical flows (particularly phosphorous and nitrogen – just look at the state of British rivers), on novel entities (you will remember plastics, pesticides and pharmaceuticals from the introduction), on land-use change, we cannot keep increasing growth in the Global North. In the UK we are using our share of the resources of three planets every year. For the US, it is five planets' worth, for Australia four and a half, overall

---

* You can locate your nearest 'Library of Things' at www.libraryofthings. co.uk.

for humanity 1.7.[5] Of course, there are nations in the Global South who need, who must have, access to more resources than now, and have absolute growth, but we in the Global North cannot. We only have one Earth.

GDP is a measure of 'the monetary value of final goods and services – that is, those that are bought by the final user – produced in a country in a given period of time'.[6] It is, in short, all the stuff where money is involved. But there are lots of things not counted in GDP. It does not count grandparents caring for grandchildren. It does not count a neighbour dropping in on a lonely older person and having a cup of tea that is the highlight of the visitee's week, and that keeps them out of hospital. It does not count the number of mature trees or wild birds or soil health.

There is an old feminist joke: 'How do you make GDP go down? Get a man to marry his housekeeper. She still does the same work but does not get paid for it anymore.' If there is a car crash on the motorway, GDP goes up – all that mechanical, and human, repair work. The pain does not get counted. If you cut down a forest, the sale of the timber raises GDP, but there is no accounting for the loss of the environmental services, or the beauty and intrinsic value of the trees. This is not real truth in bookkeeping. Only money gets counted.

Then there is the question of who benefits from the growth. We have had growth, massive growth, since the Second World War – some of which was undoubtedly necessary. Bombed buildings had to be replaced, schools updated, care homes built. And, interestingly, since the rise of neoliberalism, we have had rather less growth – the political philosophy of Margaret Thatcher and Ronald Reagan failing to deliver what it promised.

Yet that growth over decades has given us a failed society, a deeply unequal society. A few have benefited enormously, particularly since the end of the Great Levelling. Millions have been left with terrible housing; insecure, low-paid employment; poor physical and mental health; rundown, miserable communities filled with loneliness and suffering. Many more cling on to a reasonable standard of living, fearing that one personal shock – the loss of a job, a bout of ill health, a rise in interest rates – could see that plummet downwards.

There have been attempts – at least on the environmental side – to bring costs into the equation. The UK Treasury itself commissioned the Dasgupta Review in 2019, which attempted to put financial values on the services provided to the UK economy by the natural world. The independent Climate Change Committee, created by the Climate Change Act in 2008, frequently points out how dealing with the climate emergency is more financially beneficial than not. But there is a problem with this 'natural capital' approach. Put a price on something and it is up for sale – available for destruction if the price is right. You cannot put a price on something irreplaceable, and just as most people would, at least when pushed, admit that their health is priceless, so it is with our natural systems. More, there is a problem with markets, with the financialisation of any element of society. You're giving the entire society over to the financiers. There is a lot more on this in Chapter 6.

There are alternatives

Chasing growth remains the predominant political aim in most nations around the world, across most of the political spectrum. But there are exceptions. Perhaps the best known, if not exactly a model that is easy to follow, is Bhutan. The isolated mountain kingdom has long been guided by the National Happiness Index, an unfortunately 'fluffy' name perhaps, but a fine principle for putting public health and wellbeing at the core of every government decision. More relatable in the UK and US, and more explicitly focused on that wellbeing principle, is New Zealand. There the Treasury has a single document, the Living Standards Framework, which takes measures of human, natural and economic wellbeing and uses them to guide the spending decisions of the government. You might call it the common-sense approach.

This is turning around the way the British government operates, where the Treasury makes decisions for 'the economy', frequently standing in the way of essential actions on health, poverty and inequality, and the environment. A standard event in the House of Lords sees a minister at the despatch box under pressure for some departmental failing – schools not meeting the needs of students with special educational needs, or inadequate environmental reports not being delivered according to the legally mandated timetables. She or he rolls their eyes, snorts 'Treasury', and the House laughs sympathetically. The need is obvious and unchallenged, the long-term costs of not acting all too clear, but once that magic department's name is offered, that is the end of the debate. That is a nonsensical way to run a country.

Another useful international case study is Costa Rica, named by the United Nations Environment Programme as a Champion of the Earth nation and with standout health and wellbeing outcomes for its population. At the Bonn climate talks in 2017, COP23, I found myself following Costa Rica's Environment Minister Edgar Gutiérrez-Espeleta through a series of events. He received a level of adulation short only of that which might be expected for Greta Thunberg. One exchange stuck in my mind. Gutiérrez-Espeleta was asked how his nation had managed to keep pursuing renewable energy rather than fossil fuels. It was not easy, he acknowledged. Giant American companies kept lobbying politicians and the public, trying to say that 'natural' gas should be used as a 'bridging fuel'. But politicians had stood up to them, he said, backed by a public that really was convinced of the arguments, and proud of its genuinely world-leading place. Costa Rica is far from perfect – its announced aims, such as to protect 30 per cent of its seas, are not always delivered – but look at the state of its environment and the health of its people, and it is doing a lot more right than Britain.

Chapter 6
Controlling the Money

*F*inancialisation is a key symptom of the disease of neoliberalism. Institutions once run to meet human needs now have as their only goal the generation of profit for the few. The majority of people, and all of the planet, suffer.

Back before the pandemic, I got an out-of-the-blue request to meet some University of Michigan students at the Houses of Parliament. I try to say yes to such requests whenever I can, because opening up politics, making what happens in our corridors visible, is one of my projects. But this was particularly intriguing, because their master's degree subject was corruption. They had been in Paris at the headquarters of the OECD* the previous day, so they were clearly serious. And so it proved, for when I commented, as I often do, that they were sitting down the road from the standout centre of global corruption, the City of London, they just nodded acceptance of my statement as being obvious. That made me feel more hopeful about the possibilities for the future of the US: there are still functioning parts of its education system.

---

* The Organisation for Economic Co-operation and Development, whose member states are high-income countries, about 60 per cent of the global economy, broadly the more open parts of it.

The world's slow awakening

I can pinpoint my understanding of the City of London as the heart of global corruption to the reading of one book, Nicholas Shaxson's *Treasure Islands: Tax Havens and the Men Who Stole the World*, soon after its publication in 2011, and listening to a person behind a lot of its research, John Christensen, at the Camden Serious Book Club. That was how I learnt about the position of the Remembrancer, the massive funds held by the City and used for its own political purposes, and the status of the City as a political black hole at the centre of the modern capital. It is the last rotten borough where businesses – mostly financial businesses – decide the direction, and the money spent. That text sent me into the depths of the London Library, and unlikely reading in the form of *London and the Kingdom: A History Derived Mainly from the Archives at Guildhall*, printed by 'Order of the Corporation of Under the Direction of the Library Committee, 1894'. That taught me that the essential privileges of the City, in a globally unparalleled way, go back to before William the Conqueror. When the Norman invader entered the City, he promised 'not to reduce the citizens to a state of dependent vassalage, but to establish them in all the rights and privileges they had hitherto enjoyed'.

The Remembrancer is the City's rep in Parliament, with privileges to represent the financial sector and to influence legislation and MPs. There is nothing similar for nurses, for pensioners, or for any other sector of society. The City's Cash, an endowment fund run by the City of London Corporation, had an income of at least £175 million in 2021, owning giant chunks of land not just in London but also Hong Kong, New York and Sydney.[1] That is the power of compound interest over centuries, money that was originally donated for charitable purposes, when the City was a representative of a diverse economy of merchants, manufacturers and tradespeople. Now it exists, its own website used to say (it has since been changed), to promote the interests of the financial sector.

As for the rotten-borough element, that sees the votes of some 8,000 actual residents of the City concentrated in a couple of words, comprehensively trumped by the business vote of 34,000 (an imbalance increased under Tony Blair). Those elected, or rather selected, are generally the 'great and the good' – people certain not to look under any rocks for corruption. There have been attempts to elect democratic forces onto the Corporation, starting with the brave vicar William Taylor, who sought to open up the City's Cash to scrutiny. That grew with the City Reform Group in 2012, which had backing across the political spectrum as far as former Tory Home Secretary David Davis, with some success. But the maths are against the outcome that Charles II sought in 1682, trying to abolish the Corporation by influencing the election of its council.

The teens of the twenty-first century was when light was shone again on the place of the City as the representative of the financial sector. Occupy London, which had intended to set up at the centre of its turf but was pushed to the front of St Paul's Cathedral instead, in its general assembly in November 2011 demanded the abolition of the City of London and its powers (including folding its independent police force into the London Met), and a truth and reconciliation commission to examine its corruption. Those demands were not, of course, met – Occupy was by this time already running out of steam – but they set many different groups and organisations to investigating and learning about the City, work that continues to the present day.

There is nothing new about this, Charles II's efforts being followed by an 1894 Royal Commission recommendation for abolition. That approach was accepted by the prime minister of the day, Lord Rosebery. But his government fell and the Conservative Lord Salisbury reversed nearly all of the plans. The abolition of the City of London had also been post-war Labour Party policy. It was Tony Blair who removed that. That child of Thatcher I hold responsible for much of the UK's ills today; he shifted the Overton window of British politics so far to the right that the seesaw fell off its fulcrum.

Britain's weird, unwritten constitution means that the Speaker of the House of Commons could expel the Remembrancer. Caroline Lucas and I wrote to John Bercow, who was Speaker at the time, asking him to do just that. Unfortunately he said 'no'. But the Occupy movement and other stirrings had helped raise media interest and smoothed the way for extensive media coverage of a series of leaks through the decade that revealed the deep corruption, theft and abuse that is the City of London and the colonial legacy that is the UK-controlled offshore tax havens. The exemption of many of its activities from Freedom of Information legislation cannot protect it from that.

The International Consortium of Investigative Journalists has been at the centre of work on the cascade: Pandora Papers, Paradise Papers, Bahamas Leaks, Panama Papers and Offshore Leaks. This has brought a new term into the language of corruption – enablers. Activities of corrupt companies and officials are only possible because bankers, lawyers, auditors and accountants, estate agents and financial advisers find a way through a system for the corrupt. People who work in 'ordinary' sums for 'ordinary lives' know there are plenty of barriers in place to moving money or opening a bank account – multiple 'know your customer' hoops. But drug traffickers, arms traders and corrupt politicians find their way smoothly oiled.

London property prices have been pushed into the stratosphere by being used as a store for the world's illicit wealth. Russian oligarchs, enriched by the importing of neoliberal ideology from the US following the collapse of the USSR – which curiously led to an economic model looking very like nineteenth-century American robber-baron capitalism – hold houses (very rarely homes) beside properties belonging to mysteriously wealthy African oil ministers, beside Chinese technology billionaires. As an experiment, back in 2006, when I first stood for election in Regent's Park ward in Camden – an area where rundown council housing sits beside the Nash terraces facing the park – I went canvassing in the super-rich's patch. But I soon stopped, for I found myself mostly encountering bemused, and often frightened, housekeeping staff, who generally did not have a vote. Residents were almost certainly at another of their multiple homes, and their political activity contained to funding pet politicians.

Corruption is a Global North problem

That radical campaigning organisation (not) the International Monetary Fund (IMF) estimates the annual cost of corruption is $3.6 trillion – about 5 per cent of total global GDP.[2]

The bulk of that cost is borne in the Global South. The money stolen is not available for healthcare, for education, for infrastructure, and it perverts and destroys institutions that should be providing those services. (The same of course applies to tax-dodging in the UK.) The UN lists corruption as one of the chief barriers to achievement of the Sustainable Development Goals to which every nation on this planet is signed up and which none is in line to deliver.

The source of corruption is largely in the Global North. Who pays the bribe to the corrupt oil minister, or the army general commissioning wholly unnecessary military equipment? And who keeps the money for the recipient in the ironclad secrecy necessary to make the transaction possible? Swiss banking is one centre; little changed since its sickening Second World War engagement with the Nazis. Several American states and dependencies are prominent, but the UK is, in this area, truly world-leading. The functioning of the City of London and its ilk can only be described as one of the continuing key levers of neocolonialism. A few nations (and a few people within them) profit while the rest of them pay.

That corruption is not contained in the financial sector, but pervasive in our political institutions. Who pays – particularly in the US and the UK – for the politics we get? The fossil-fuel producers, the financial sector, the gun industry in the US, the pharmaceutical industry, gambling firms and alcohol-makers. They fund our political parties, directly and indirectly, and decide which candidates will represent them.

As a respondent on Twitter noted as I commented on the list of donations to the Tory Party candidates in the race to replace Boris Johnson, how is any payment not corruption? No one pays money without expecting a return – and it does not have to be as blatant as property developer Richard Desmond's interactions with the Tory Party's Housing Secretary Robert Jenrick. We get the politics the few pay for – and the consequent deregulation and open slather of corruption, environmental destruction, poverty and inequality.

Ministers meet often with the well-funded lobbyists of the multinational companies, while non-governmental organisations and citizens' advocates struggle for the occasional crumb of time. Austerity – cutting back in the civil service – has greatly broadened the always well-oiled revolving door between the public and private sectors. Former secretaries of state get extraordinarily ill-defined, lucrative 'jobs' as advisers and board members once they leave office. Dubious autocratic states funding luxurious travel for MPs gets a fair bit of attention, but it is a tiny fraction of the issue of corruption in our government and Parliament.

Too much finance

Always, whether it is funding continuing hugely publicly subsidised oil and gas development (despite various promises to end the cash handouts for these indefensible benefit recipients), or storing money for oligarchs and dictators, right in the middle of the mess is the financial sector. Which has, in the UK, managed to carve a notably prominent place for itself in the national story. Gordon Brown's infamous Mansion House speech of 2007 proclaiming a 'new golden age for the City of London' is remembered now chiefly for its timing. It was just before the global financial crash, where the 'talent', 'flexibility' and 'adaptability' this Labour prime minister lauded saw us coming within hours of the cash machines stopping working. But it deserves analysis on a broader scale – as a sign of the pervasive dominance of the financial sector.

An International Monetary Fund working paper from 2012 has given name to a phenomenon increasingly acknowledged: that the world – and particularly the UK – suffer from 'too much finance'. It was, weirdly enough, at an economics conference in Croatia that I saw Professor Tim Jackson present a graph that for me has always crystallised the problem. It showed where money for bank loans from the UK was going – predominantly back into the financial sector itself, with a large chunk also going into housing, jacking up the prices.* Only about 10 per cent went into the 'real' economy, funding small businesses, manufacturers, the businesses providing the goods and services we actually need and want. This circular economy (in the worst sense – only the few benefit) is 8.6 per cent of national GDP, and half of London's, helping explain the city's place as home to the richest and some of the poorest local government areas in Europe.

The Green alternative is a financial sector that serves the needs of the real economy, not circulating the extraordinary sums it does now within itself. It should simply be a place to store money, to loan funds for useful activities, to be a boring utility, not a site of speculation and extraordinary profit. That Green alternative would also free a huge amount of human resources for productive, useful purposes. Many PhD

---

* The New Economics Foundation produced a brilliant paper in 2016, *The Financialisation of UK Homes* (neweconomics.org/2016/04/the-financialisation-of-uk-homes), demonstrating how loosening of loan provision was the chief factor in soaring, unaffordable house prices.

graduates in physics, maths and many other subjects, and some of the highest-scoring undergraduates, go into finance, into the maw of the machine of abusively long working hours and £1,000 bottles of champagne. That has a massive opportunity cost. Those human talents could be going into manufacturing, farming, the NHS, many other sectors that urgently need the social innovation they could be bending their brains towards. Instead, it is all for the empty goal of more moneymaking for the few.

Meanwhile, banks are irrelevant to large parts of the economy. In 2013 I was on a visit to North Yorkshire as Green Party leader, talking to the founder of an innovative restaurant who had helped make his small town a gourmet centre. I asked him, already guessing the answer, where the finance to start the business had come from. 'Was it a bank?' The tone of his laughing response – 'Of course not' – was bitter. Like so many similar businesses, he had managed to scrape together savings, loans from family and friends, put his entire life on the line, to get the business going. People without that social capital never start their business idea, or it fails early for lack of funding.

A banking sector regionalised, localised, with credit unions, building societies and small local banks that know the area, that would see their role as being to support their area, would be a very different and far more productive financial sector than our current arrangements, and a foundation of a secure and resilient society. The many failures of banks to meet consumers' and businesses' basic needs, to treat them with decency, respect and compassion, fills acres of newsprint every week. Yet there was massive resistance when I was part of a push in the House of Lords to get a 'duty of care' (led by that hardly radical organisation Macmillan Cancer Support) into a finance bill.

Where is the competition?

The interests of finance are now to be found in almost every corner of every aspect of life on this planet. It was on World Food Day 2018, listening to Canadian academic Jennifer Clapp speaking at the University of Sheffield, that this issue was first clearly framed for me. Her focus is on the food sector. She set out how each part of the chain – seed and agrichemical companies, manufacturers, fast-food retailers and supermarkets – have shrunk from around seven companies dominating their market to even fewer. The pattern is clear, from seeds and chemicals (Bayer/Monsanto, Dow/DuPont, ChemChina, Syngenta and BASF), to production (ADM, Bunge, Cargill, Louis Dreyfus), to processing (Kraft/Heinz, Nestlé, Dr Pepper/Snapple/Keurig/Green Mountain, AB InBev, Pepsi), to retail (Walmart, Asda/Sainsbury's, Tesco/Kroger, Loblaws and Shoppers, Amazon and Wholefoods).

But the lack of diversity – so unhealthy in any kind of system – goes even further than the big names. For as Clapp illustrates, the ownership of those big names is largely with a handful of players. The five largest asset-management firms own typically 10 to 20 per cent of each of the major players. If significant ownership is shared across all of the major actors in a sector, where is the competition? If we're looking for an explanation for the recent burst of inflation – when wages have not been going up but prices have, in ways far from fully explicable by energy price hikes – then here is one.

Recently, this issue has hit social media, with a range of actors sharing the broad claim that BlackRock and Vanguard (two such asset-management firms) own 'all the biggest corporations in the world'. Among the companies listed are Apple, Facebook, Lockheed Martin, Tesla, MasterCard, DuPont, General Electric, Fox, Disney, Microsoft, Paramount and IBM. It is an interesting measure of our times that both BlackRock and Vanguard both felt the need to respond to Reuters about the postings, saying, as the news agency put it, 'While they do appear to own significant shares in the world's biggest businesses, those shares are purchased using money belonging to their clients – and therefore the shareholders are ultimately their clients.'[3] Which is, rather obviously, missing the point. The shareholders have given decision-making over the use of their money to the asset-management firms, so they have a huge influence.

For many years there has been a common left-wing political trope of pointing out that giant multinational companies, assessed by market capitalisation, would fit on global lists alongside national GDPs. One such study in 2021 found Apple ranking eighth in the world, and Microsoft tenth, both above Russia, Canada, Brazil and South Korea. Amazon is about the same level as those nations. The degree of power over national governments that this gives has long been of concern – but what about companies that have an interest in all of the multinational giants? The annual letter that BlackRock's Larry Fink writes to CEOs gets considerably more media coverage than most pronouncements from the UN Secretary General – and is equally political, without any kind of mandate except that of pure, raw cash. He used 2022's letter to say BlackRock would not be pressing for fossil-fuel divestment.

Beware the bubble popping

Finance thinks short-term, and in the current times that is not just environmentally disastrous, but also incredibly economically risky. A single organisation, the Carbon Tracker Initiative, has done a huge amount to highlight the financial risks attached to a reality identified by the International Energy Agency, which says we have to leave at least two-thirds of known fossil-fuel reserves in the ground if we are to avoid catastrophic climate change. Ten years after it started its work, the problem has only grown, with its latest estimate being that at least $1 trillion of oil and gas assets[4], mostly listed on the major global stock markets, risk being stranded as the world finally, as it must, delivers on climate action.

A global financial crash on a scale never previously seen, caused by a sudden recognition of the issue, would be one way to cut carbon, but not a good way. We do not get to a sustainable economy by crashing and burning the current one. Stopping burning things, in metaphoric as well as physical ways, is the Green alternative, but allowing unstable, volatile financial considerations to dominate decisions about our lives is one sure way to set a bonfire of economic disaster and human suffering.

Unpayable debt

At the end of 2022, global total debt leverage – public and private – had reached a new record level, 349 per cent of annual global GDP, or $37,500 of debt per person.[5] It is a figure I have been tracking for years, with growing concern. During the aftermath of the global financial crash of 2007–8, Greece's national figure reaching little more than half of that caused international conniptions. The most recent jump was of course pandemic-related, but this only reflects a long-term trend.

It is clear that this money is unpayable under current arrangements. When you put this together with the level of environmental destruction, we're laying a huge weight on the future. Professor Steve Keen is one of the few economists I have seen really trying to tackle this issue, which was why I invited him to speak at a Green Party conference in 2016. His proposal then was to revive a modified form of traditional regular debt forgiveness. Such cancellation was central in Jewish and early Christian thinking, and surely needs to be revisited. Professor Keen's proposal was to pay what is often known as 'helicopter money' – deposits of cash – to every member of society. Those with debt would have to use the money to pay it off, while those without would have the cash. That would remove what is often seen as a 'moral hazard', that the profligate and well-connected benefit most if debt is simply forgiven.

What is money?

This is where I need to take a little detour into the nature of money. Many years ago, I was a volunteer at the British Museum in the money gallery, where visitors could experience many forms of ancient and historic currency – from blocks of tea from the Silk Road to early modern English hammered coins. As part of that training, we were told the curators had planned to have a single 'What is money?' sentence at the entrance to the gallery. But they could not find a simple enough explanation, so there was none. Essentially, money is whatever a society decides it is. Cleopatra – yes *that* Cleopatra – created an entirely token currency, where the value of the metal in the coins bore no relationship to the face. Now, of course, most money does not have any physical form at all.

Since the global financial crash, there has been mass-scale 'printing of money' – quantitative easing, a key factor in the explosion of inequality as asset prices have leapt up to absorb that money. Then came Covid, and to fund its rescue measures, the British government 'borrowed' £413 billion between March 2020 and July 2021, at the same time as the Bank of England purchased £412 billion in government debt – 99.5 per cent of the total.[6] What if we just wrote that off? We would not be poorer; the only loss would be the interest on the loan, which was going to the government anyway.

That would be in line with a fast-rising heterodox area of economics called Modern Monetary Theory, among whose chief proponents has been Stephanie Kelton, an academic who advised Bernie Sanders during his presidential run. I am not going to get into the depths of the theory here – there is definitely plenty to be found on the internet – but essentially it allows for a lot more deficit funding, governments spending money on things society needs, than old, traditional economics.

Crucially, in the UK, it is a break from the ridiculously outdated Thatcherite idea that national spending is like that of a single household – that you have to balance taxes in with spending out. The difference is, of course, that a household could try to print its own money, but would find it impossible to get anyone to accept it. Unlike a state. The 'rules' of finance, of markets, are not like the rules of physics. They are an entirely human creation. They can be shaped differently, if we choose.

How do we take on the financial sector?

That really is the multitrillion-dollar question. Finance has an enormous hold on our politics, our economy, our society; over centuries society has been increasingly arranged for its benefit, the trap of debt holding many individuals very firmly in its grasp. It would be possible to write a history of the last few hundred years as the triumph of the City of London (as *Treasure Islands*, to a degree, does). It is notable that when I was elected as leader of the Green Party in 2012, the only coverage in the *Evening Standard*, London's then influential evening newspaper, was in the finance diary section, noting my opposition to the City of London Corporation.

But it has been taken on before and reined in. After the Great Depression, in the United States there was a significant tightening of controls of the financial sector; de-risking that also helped reduce inequality. It was gradually undone in the couple of decades to 2007. There were strong controls on the UK sector until Margaret Thatcher's Big Bang deregulation of 1983. The dominance of the financial sector – and its dangerous instability – are the result of political choices. We can make different choices.

I come back to a chant I have joined – and led – on many

a political march: 'We are the many, they are the few.' Forcing big money out of politics, bringing in state funding for political parties and ending donations beyond crowdfunding levels would take away a huge amount of financial-sector power. That should be combined with strict rules preventing politicians and civil servants from cashing in after they leave office, the implicit quid pro quo so evident in current decision-making. That would take us much closer to a democracy making decisions for the people, rather than for finance. Everything in the end comes back to democracy.

Practical steps

This one small section could be a book all of its own, but here are some of the big steps, and illustration that there is a lot of thought going into alternatives to our current model, and routes to getting there.

Possibly the biggest single step towards slashing the damage done by the financial sector would be closing down the tax havens and cutting their links with the City of London – ending the loopholes through which the enablers guide their clients. There have been tentative and inadequate steps in that direction – most recently in forcing registration of who really owns property in the UK held under overseas ownership (typically through opaque property arrangements). There is a huge distance to go, but the starting point has to be having a government that really *wants* to act on these issues.

Also crucial would be getting finance out of places where it obviously does not belong. In the past year in the UK there is pretty well a national consensus that finance does not belong in the water sector, a case study of awful privatisation of which there is now acute awareness. Care homes and the NHS, energy suppliers, railways . . . there is a long list of places where a majority of the public are clear that running essential services for private profit rather than public good has been a disaster.

And in turning the financial sector into a tool of the real economy, one long-time idea, known as a Tobin tax, would be a powerful one. That means putting a tax on every financial transaction, gumming up the works of the gameplaying, gambling sides of finance. Also we need to end autonomous machine trading (where the person with the fastest computer and link wins), the dangerous instability of which is being increasingly recognised after a succession of 'flash crashes'. When the algorithm is in charge, we all lose. You might also have heard of a similar idea, the 'Robin Hood tax'. Rather than aiming to cut the number of transactions, it wants to take a little of the profit from every transaction and put it towards good causes. That is better than allowing the speculators to scoop up the lot, but still leaves the financial sector to run rampant.

Rebalancing the power

We have got some powerful new tools in this political struggle. Social media, and the electronic nature of modern finance, mean, as the cascade of leaks has shown, keeping a secret these days is far harder than in the past. The shadowy foundations of finance are being exposed. And various forms of heterodox economics are getting increasing traction.

There is also a powerful push from geopolitics. After the Russian invasion of Ukraine, and with China taking a newly hawkish world view, concern about the impact of those countries' nationals, and those from other autocracies, has risen to the surface. In the House of Lords we had a very powerful, and surprisingly consensual, debate called by former Labour defence secretary, Lord (Des) Browne of Ladyton on 'the impact on global democratic norms and values from autocrats, kleptocrats and populists and the case for a coordinated response by the United Kingdom and her allies'. The role of financial enablers in supporting and assisting these regimes and their leaders was widely accepted as a grave cause for concern.

And what you might call the 'intelligent end' of the current system is increasingly recognising its unsustainability. The *Financial Times* has led the way in highlighting the damage done by financialisation of the water and care sectors in particular – and also has its advocates for universal basic income, or at least the exploration thereof. *The Economist* has been known to say the political power of the fossil-fuel sector needs to be reined in to tackle the climate emergency.

But ultimately, we have to come back to a Thatcherite phrase – 'there is no alternative'. If the financial sector is not reined in, it will destroy the foundations on which it is built. There are no jobs on a dead planet. On a financialised planet there is eventually no real economy. Duelling computer algorithms cannot exist without electricity, without society and a functional planet, without people having sustainable lives.

Part C
Healthy Life

Chapter 7
Enabling Wellbeing

The vast bulk of discussion of health, and the overwhelming majority of health funding, goes towards seeking treatments for illness. Only the crumbs of resources, the dedicated and committed, are focused on keeping people well. That approach leaves us with a profoundly diseased society.

Walk the streets of the financial centre of the City of London, or an expensive suburb of Manchester, and you would think the National Health Service was doing a great job, living up to its name – fit, active men in their sixties striding out, young women visibly glowing with health, with the flexible limbs of a yoga or Pilates fan. The NHS, much loved and much celebrated – see the opening ceremony of the 2012 London Olympic Games featuring dancing doctors and nurses and Great Ormond Street Hospital – is clearly doing its job, living up to its name.

Visit, however, the aisles of Sheffield's traditional market, or walk the streets of Somers Town, the old railway workers' centre in central London, and you would doubt that conclusion. The level of ill health is achingly visible, and unavoidable: the tired-looking, obese woman in her forties on a mobility scooter, the young man hunched over a crutch with a complicated brace whose bolts go into a badly smashed-up leg,

the street drinker or 'spice' user with prematurely aged face
and bandaged ulcers. Few people will look actively healthy;
most will look worn down by life.

When I was chair of the local community group trying to
stop construction of the Francis Crick (medical research)
Institute in Somers Town, a local government official was
trying to sway me and the audience. 'Think of what wonderful high-tech treatments might be discovered here to extend
lifespan.' My response was mediated only by the fact that
you do not verbally beat up officials promoting their political bosses' policy (in this case Labour's). But it would have
been, in vehement tones, that decent housing, local employment opportunities and healthy food would do far more for
life expectancy in Somers Town than high-tech medicine,
there only for when people are already suffering disabling
conditions.

That personal observation is backed up by the statistics. In
2018, female life expectancy in the UK was 83.1, more than
two years below the OECD average, putting the UK twenty-
fifth out of thirty-eight nations. For the fifth largest economy
in the world, that is poor. But far worse is the inequality. In
the poorest 10 per cent of local government wards in the
country, female life expectancy at birth was 78.7 years; in
national figures only Mexico was lower. By contrast, in the
richest 10 per cent of wards, the life expectancy is 86.4 years,
below only the national figure for the famously long-lived
Japan. That one statistic identifies that the UK has massive
health problems caused by inequality.[1]

A key element of the ideology of the past century is that
as human beings we can always expect to be going forward.
Yet on the measure that most people aim for, healthy life

expectancy, the UK is at best stalling, and, in some of the poorest areas of the country, going significantly backwards. In Scotland, in the three years to 2020 it fell for men by a year, in the East Midlands by 9.6 months. A girl born today in Blackpool could expect to live twenty-three fewer healthy years than one in the Orkney Islands. Blackpool's figures really are shocking – overall healthy life expectancy for men of 62.8 years, for women 63.6. Of course, that is not to say – for the avoidance of doubt – that a life lived in ill health cannot still be full, rewarding and contributory – but we would all hope for better than that. (And when I look at the House of Lords, which you might suggest as a definition of privilege, there are a lot of members doing far better than that in healthy, active lifespan.)

Free at the point of use

Nonetheless, that no one in the UK has – or until recently has had – to worry about a medical bill is one of the great successes of the post-Second World War political settlement. And once you're ill, the NHS has high-tech treatments and the latest in research-backed approaches as good as anything anywhere. The NHS was ranked by the Commonwealth Fund as top of eleven major health systems around the world in 2017.[2]

And the alternative to free-at-the-point-of-use is terrifying. Many years ago, in the early days of the internet, when I was based in Bangkok, I enjoyed being part of an American-dominated community of copyeditors brought together by a simple email list. About half the traffic from them was anxious queries about health insurance: which jobs had it, what it did and did not cover. I remember one heart-wrenching account from that time of a young couple – married as graduate students, as Americans often are. One was becoming obviously, seriously ill. But they had to wait for tests until she had graduated and got a job with spouse health cover. (Imagine the stress of the job interviews.) It turned out to be liver cancer. He died. Maybe he would have died even with immediate treatment, but think of the suffering and worry, whatever the outcome – that is a market-based, wealth-rationed healthcare system.

The outcomes of that US system are predictably awful. The Commonwealth Fund's 2021 study puts, on a range of measures, its results last of eleven high-income countries, despite it spending nearly 17 per cent of GDP on healthcare. That contrasts to France, Germany and Canada, on around 11 per cent. In absolute spending terms, the difference is even more stark. A comparison is often made with Costa Rica, a high-health, middle-income country. It spends only about a tenth of the money per person on healthcare as the US, and gets significantly better outcomes. Yet the UK has imported, to the highest positions, managers who have worked in, and proselytised for, the US system, and brought in US companies (often with dreadful reputations) to provide services for the NHS. There is nothing in the model to copy, yet that is the path large parts of our political class – Tory and Labour – are set on.

Read the accounts of what life was like for many in pre-NHS Britain, and the UK was much like the modern US. David Kynaston's brilliant *Austerity Britain: 1945–1951* (part of a series well worth reading, and bestsellers despite their weight) reports on the experience of Dr Alistair Clark, an 'ordinary' GP. When treatment was made free: 'For the first six months I had as many as 20 or 30 ladies come to me who had the most unbelievable gynaecological conditions . . . at least 10 who had complete prolapse of their womb, and they had to hold it up with a towel as if they had a large nappy on.' Let's not go back there. Healthcare free at the point of use, provision according to need, is clearly exactly the right approach.

NHS in trouble

That cautionary tale means I always pause before talking about the NHS's troubles. It is something right-wing commentators often do as a prelude for calling for privatisation of our health services, or at least the ending or cutting back on services free at the point of use. 'We cannot afford it any more,' they say. To which the first answer is easy: we created the NHS at the end of the Second World War, when Britain had been impoverished by the financial, physical and human costs of the global conflict, was laden with debt and desperately low on national income. If we can create the NHS under those conditions, surely we can continue it today?

But the principle keeps being nibbled away at. We saw Rishi Sunak in the Tory leadership election suggesting that patients should be charged for missing appointments, as if those likely to be hit were not already the most vulnerable – the single mum whose bus never turned up, the drug addict struggling to get their life together. 'Free at the point of use' is attacked as a principle with increasing frequency. Former health secretary (then chancellor) Jeremy Hunt, in a 2005

book brought together by then Tory (later UKIP) MP Douglas Carswell, and also backed by Michael Gove and Kwasi
Kwarteng, called for an insurance-based system. That Hunt
later disavowed the proposal is more a demonstration of the
political power of the idea of the NHS than anything else.

But it is unarguable that the NHS today is in deep difficulties, tottering at the point of being overwhelmed – that
needs to be confronted. Having, just about, got through the
acute crisis of the coronavirus pandemic, it is struggling –
and often failing – to meet demand, with waiting times in
accident and emergency departments and waiting lists for
operations heading into the stratosphere. As I write in
summer 2023, more than 7 million people in England are on
a waiting list for treatment,[3] around one in ten people. Half
of those have been waiting for more than a year.

The rise of 'going private'

'Free at the point of use' in a timely manner is increasingly
not the case, not just for exotic, extreme treatments that the
overseeing body, NICE (the National Institute for Health
and Care Excellence), has declined to support (sometimes for
good reason). Crowdfunding for those has been happening
ever since the technique was invented. But, increasingly,
there are appeals for standard provision: an electric wheel-
chair, a hip operation for someone who cannot bear the
waiting list any longer, a child whose local trust does not
provide a service available elsewhere.

Understandably, that means use of private health insurance is growing, and many people are digging into their

savings – or borrowing – to jump the queue. That means on average £13,000 for a knee replacement; cataract surgery £3,000. But private services generally only cover the relatively straightforward. Private hospitals do not have intensive-care facilities. Should your operation go wrong, the cost will be transferred to the NHS. And medical professionals are usually trained in the NHS before transferring for some or all of their time to the private sector. So the pressure on the NHS grows, and the funding for the simpler procedures goes private.

Underlying the waiting lists is long-term underspending. Historically, the UK in total spent between 1 and 1.5 percentage points of GDP less on health than Germany and France. The costs of patching the gaping holes – notably for agency staff – has lifted that in the past couple of years, but there is a huge long-term deficit in spending. And several percentage points are private spending, far less efficient than public.

Not pulling our weight

But also, increasingly, there are acute staffing shortages in the NHS. The funds to pay medical professionals and other staff are available, but the staff are not. Brexit is a big issue there, but above all is the issue of staff retention. Covid was a huge blow – staff across the board are exhausted, but they are also fed up with low pay, and simple lack of respect. It is a rare case, but government is actually on track to deliver its election promise for recruiting new nurses. However, the rate of attrition is such that there has been no progress on the shortage.

The staffing shortage is a long-term historic issue. Charing Cross Hospital recently unveiled a mural commemorating nine African women's contributions to healthcare in the UK, going back through the twentieth century. But it was after the Second World War that the UK began the wholesale importing of doctors, nurses and other medical professionals from the fading empire and then the Commonwealth, then from Europe and other parts of the Global South. We have not, in recent history, trained anything like enough medical professionals, and generally rely on far poorer countries, effectively stealing their resources. Some nations, the Philippines being the standout example, do train people explicitly 'for export', although there are real questions to be asked about the social impact of women, who often have children, leaving them to raise essential funds for their family and nation by bringing their professional skills to the UK.

There is a global shortage of medical professionals. Some of the people we train will inevitably choose to go elsewhere. We should be training more professionals than we need, but instead, in 2022 only 54 per cent of doctors joining the health service came from the UK.[4] For new nurses it was less than 50 per cent.[5] That a wealthy country like Britain should be pulling its weight – needs to pull its weight – in medical training is only common sense.

Open and stealth privatisations

Kynaston reports that in the early days of the NHS the biggest pressures were on 'drugs, spectacles and false teeth'. That those were all provided free but have been largely taken away has almost been forgotten. The Green alternative, common sense, is that all of these, so crucial to people living full, healthy lives, must be returned under full NHS cover. Preventing people from getting this basic healthcare is bad for all of us.

But the privatisation is not just in limited areas of service. Seven per cent of the spend in the NHS now is going direct to private companies for the provision of services, everything from GP clinics to mental health (an area where public provision has been particularly heavily cut). Entirely typical was the sale in late 2020 of a group of local doctors' surgeries in North London, serving 370,000 patients, taken over, after minutes of consideration by the local clinical commissioning group, by Centene, on its own account 'the leading provider of NHS primary care services in the UK'.[6] It also ranked at the time as the forty-second-richest US corporation. In September 2023, the future of the services was thrown into doubt when Centene decided to sell them, essential services being treated as financial assets, lives traded for profit.

I joined for one day the '999 Call for the NHS' new Jarrow March* in 2014, my diary dictating that it be the leg between Bedford and Luton. When this sometimes limping, traffic-deafened group straggled into a pub en route, the young man behind the bar asked, 'Why are you here?' 'We're protesting against the privatisation of the NHS,' came our well-rehearsed reply. 'Are they privatising it? I have not seen it,' was the surprised response. That reflects most public

---

* It was modelled on the Jarrow March (also known as the Jarrow Crusade) of 1936, a protest against unemployment and poverty.

understanding. While Virgin Healthcare might have been operating your local GP clinic – making profit from catering to your needs – the sign above the door still says NHS.

The creeping privatisation might have gone further had it not been for the cautionary tale – for the private sector as much as the public – of Hinchingbrooke Hospital. It was handed to Circle to run in 2012, and handed back by it in 2015 after a damning inspection report on the dangerously poor quality of services it was providing. Like the debacle of the 2012 Olympics – when multinational oppression giant G4S got the security contract, then failed to spend enough on staff and the military had to step in – it is a demonstration of one of the key issues with privatisation: if things go wrong on critical provision, it will always be the state that has to step in to pick up the pieces.

Social-care disaster

Healthcare is following the disastrous path of social care, in both care homes and in-home provision, a privatisation now so fully entrenched that it has become almost invisible. That was until the fragility, instability and danger of the financialisation of the sector became evident. The NHS was truly world-leading in the quality of what was called 'geriatric care' until the 1980s, when the government began withdrawing from provision of care for older and disabled and vulnerable people, leaving it to charitable and, increasingly, for-profit providers. The number of private residential-home places increased from 44,000 in 1982 to 164,000 in 1994.[7] This had the impact of shifting the costs of frailty, illness and disability from all of us, as shared through the state, so we jointly carry the risk, to individuals.

The Blair and Brown governments did nothing to reverse this privatisation, indeed they allowed or encouraged it to continue. That brings us to the current day, where in 2021 the hedge-fund and private-equity owners were taking out of the 'care' sector £1.5 billion a year in rent, debt payments and fees. And complaining that they could not afford to pay their workers an increase in the minimum wage.

The profit motive has no place in care

The Green position is very different from that of other political forces in the UK. Health and social care should not be supplied by for-profit organisations. Privatisation of any services is built on cutting the pay and conditions of workers, as well as the quality of services, and pumping public money into private hands. That is pernicious in any area, but particularly in care, which should be guided by compassion, by need, by humanity.

Put profit into the equation, and what kind of choices do you get? A nurse caring for two dying patients at the same time would be more profitable than one-to-one care. An abused child can be cared for more cheaply by a low-paid casual worker, who will be here today and gone tomorrow. A skilled psychologist working with a patient with a drug addiction is far more expensive than a group session of follow-the-formula therapy. Society pays with huge levels of suffering, but the hedge funds just keep raking in the profits.

Drug and vaccine companies

The profit motive is equally destructive when it comes to medicines, vaccines and medical devices. New antibiotics are not being developed, despite the existentially urgent need for them, on a planet where these lifesaving drugs are thrown into the environment, particularly on factory farms, with careless abandon. There is no money to be made. But Viagra, well, that was a real money-spinner, as are drugs for the chronic diseases of the Global North, which patients will take for a lifetime, even if the benefits for some are doubtful, at best.*

But the misdirection of research towards moneymaking drugs rather than the most medically crucial is only the start of the problem. A recent fascinating study on Alzheimer's disease showed that rate of decline in patients was slowed by the 'prescription' of regular video calls – simply the chance for social interaction.[8] Yet drug companies have been chasing, with a notable lack of success, drugs for the condition for decades.

Treatments from which no or little profit can be made do not get researched, do not even get thought about. Herbal and traditional remedies are frequently dismissed as 'not researched'. But why not? Because not enough money can be made, and the best brains, the fanciest laboratories, all of the power of the modern economy, is directed not towards health, but to lucrative treatments.

---

* For much more on this see Ben Goldacre's *Bad Pharma: How Drug Companies Mislead Doctors and Harm*.

The Green alternative: building a healthy society

Back in 2015 in Manchester, I gave a keynote address at the International Festival of Public Health. As I looked at the speech I had drafted, just before standing up, I had a moment of panic: was not I just telling an audience of specialists what their speciality was, and that the UK was doing very badly at it, something they well knew? But I should not have worried. The speech – pointing out that poor housing, low pay and long working hours, exam stress and rigid schooling systems, polluted environments and lack of opportunities to exercise were all health issues needing urgent attention – went down a treat. That a political party got the nature of public health, that health is not just about treating disease, and that we are trapped with most focus, attention and funding going to what is essentially a National Illness Service was a revelation for the audience. It was clear they had never heard this from a politician before. (And I was delighted that they invited me back in 2023.)

Some of the challenges facing the NHS are demographic. The ageing population will create more issues, more demand. But it is the level of ill-health, physical and mental, the impossibility of a doctor solving overcrowded, damp housing, or inadequate income and food-preparation time leading to an ultra-processed diet, that is at the core of the challenge to the NHS. It cannot fix much of what ails us, just as we cannot expect schools to 'fix' the attainment gap between poorest and richest pupils.

In 2023 there was a great deal of commentary on the reality that the UK had seen rates of participation in paid labour – the percentage of working-age people in or looking for paid work – collapse not just during Covid, but afterwards, reusing the old phrase for the 'Ottoman Empire', 'the sick man of Europe'. Often this was being attributed to the 'collapse of the NHS'; the deeply unhealthy structure of our society did not get a mention.

Greens understand that health does not come from treating illness but from preventing it in the first place. The NHS can do useful work – on smoking cessation, on green prescribing (such as free swimming-pool visits or outdoor activities) – but the bulk of the job of making the UK a healthy society lies in other policy areas. Ensure people's houses, jobs and diet do not make them ill and you will hugely cut the demand for healthcare: that is common sense.

Healthcare as a human right

Far too often, when thinking about different ways of doing things, we fail to look outside the Anglo-Saxon world. When it comes to health, Cuba is one place that truly is world-leading, despite many other political problems. Following the hideous late Spanish colonial period, when perhaps 10 per cent of the population died as the colonialists tried to starve out rebels, a healthy population was seen as a weapon against colonists (the USA after the Spanish).[9] The 1940 constitution was the first in the world to establish good public health and healthcare as a basic right. And just like a universal basic income, that is common sense: what is a right to life without a right to healthcare? That is something we, and most other countries in the world, are signed up to through the World Health Organization charter: 'the highest attainable standard of health' as a fundamental right.

Chapter 8
Unleashing Culture

To demonstrate that a different world is possible, we need to imagine it; to allow painters, novelists, craftspeople to help us create it, not just in art galleries and the homes of the wealthy, but in the fabric of everyone's daily life. Culture should be something you do and live, not just buy from a multinational supplier.

'It was better under Thatcher' were words I never expected to hear at a Green Party conference, but I did in autumn 2018, at a fringe event discussing the benefits of universal basic income for the creative sector. The speaker was referring to one specific policy, the Enterprise Allowance Scheme, which provided a payment set slightly above the unemployment benefit, going to people who were starting their own business or developing their career as an artist. They could briefly outline their plan, then go away for a year and try to put it into action. No regular reporting, no hassling to apply for other jobs they were not suited for and probably would not get. And that often came on top of the student grant (not loan!) for university or art college, and with very cheap or free (squat) housing.

When the Blair government came in, a new 'contract for welfare' started us down the path to the awful 'strivers versus skivers' rhetoric of the 2000s. No longer was there support for a budding musician or artist, playwright or author. No wonder the *New Music Express* (*NME*) devoted a major part of an issue in 1998 to featuring everyone from Jarvis Cocker to Bobby Gillespie, Pete Voss of Campag Velocet to Alan McGee (who had been with his protegés Oasis to No. 10 soon after Blair's election) to express their disgust. The Verve's collective statement sums it up: 'The way things work in a band is not like any other job – you have to be ready before you can earn any wages. How can you get ready if you have to graft six days a week? You'd never have the time or the energy.' Universal basic income allows that time and energy.

I am not a natural commentator on music. I can only clap in time to the rhythm if I have got someone to watch. I was thrown out of the primary-school choir for being tuneless. So when I was asked as party leader to give a keynote address at a national community music festival, my partner was horrified. 'You're not going to try to talk about music, are you?' I did not. Except when I commented on my tone-deafness, and got a chorus back of 'there's no such thing'. I talked instead about grassroots and community theatre – based on my years of experience as a reviewer in London, in part as a community service, in part because it got me free tickets. (You can still find mylondonyourlondon.com out there, looking very old WordPress.) I talked about how inspiring and wonderful it was to see so many productions put on in 'a room behind a pub' (like the White Bear in South London), and how the Camden People's Theatre aimed to live up to its name. And I would now add the brilliant Theatre Deli in Sheffield to that list.

Culture as what you do, not just what you buy

Talking about grassroots theatre allowed me to illustrate a core principle of Green creative policy – that culture should be something the majority of people have the chance to create themselves, to be involved in, or at least see in their local community hall or at an outdoor theatre in their local park. That is instead of the only option being a glossy, shiny production by the few: subscriptions on Netflix or the Disney Channel, a megastar at a giant stadium or the Royal Shakespeare Company (much as I am a fan).

Of course the local production is not the same thing as the glossy multinational. I did once get into trouble with a My London reader who, on the strength of my recommendation, took his children, who were studying *Hamlet*, to the White Bear production. Having seen an RSC effort, they were 'very disappointed'. But that father was missing the point, had swallowed the idea that the only value was in the most polished, most star-filled, performance. The experience of sitting in two rows of rickety seats watching Shakespeare performed in your face in a zero-budget format is much closer to the original experience (you might have had a stool on stage then). And the cost is a tiny fraction of the RSC version, is quite likely very local to you, and it is just possible that one day one of these young, just-starting-out actors will be on the RSC boards at Stratford-upon-Avon as a star. It is accessible, and different from the RSC, not inferior.

Boring!

So many of the high-end cultural experiences now on offer, promoted expensively at every turn – the Netflix or Disney mega-series, the manufactured TV talent-show pop star and the virtual 'reality' series, the latest novel from a star genre writer or the art-gallery blockbuster show – are polished to the point of blandness, even the 'shocking bits' fitting a formula. It is so generic that the sequel, and prequel, and every other frantic reworking of previously successful models is stuck in a zero-sum game. Breakthroughs often come from the fringe, edgy and raw. But that is soon appropriated and smoothed into just another product. It is designed to be addictive, as ultra-processed food is designed, but it is also unsatisfying. How often do you talk to a friend regretting spending a weekend binge-watching the latest hit series, who emerged feeling they have wasted that time?

That is true of mass media, but even more obvious on social media, where the influencers, the stars, the sudden smash hits, are carefully selected by the algorithm, for the interests of a range of the most economically useful people. Start watching TikTok videos about culinary uses for wild-flowers, dogs demonstrating their intelligence, and yoga positions that are good for the hips (okay, I am giving away personal preferences here), and you will soon have a feed full of similar.

You will not get the unexpected pleasures to be found in wandering into a local pub and finding a band of a genre you would never have sought out, and having a whale of a time. Or going to a local shopping centre and finding a street acrobat who leaves your children asking, 'How did they do that and can I do it too?' Or sitting in a community garden watching the children dash around a creative sculpture, exploring its textures and testing how it changes the views. A burst of music, a beautiful image, an inspiring poem on a street corner – these enrich all of our lives: that is common sense.

Enriching communities

Visiting continental Europe, I am often struck by how much art there is enmeshed in everyday life – in the small suburban shopping centre, on buses and trams, on social housing and in small villages. The UK is severely art-deprived, and that needs to change; it could improve the quality of all of our lives. The dreadful state of architecture will come up in the next chapter, but it can certainly be improved and enlivened by the addition of creativity. What we have in the UK tends to be at major institutions, in the centre of the biggest cities, and chosen to be as inoffensive as possible. *Paradigm*, the stack of metal tetrahedra in front of the Crick Institute, outside St Pancras station, is my go-to example. It is supposed to illustrate a theory of scientific discovery and 'reflect the ambitions of the institute'. Its emotional resonance is zero, its impact on its surroundings ditto.

The Green alternative is art in every local park and community garden, in schools and community centres, made to delight, enrich, engage. What does that look like? My case study is the absolutely wonderful Green Backyard in Peterborough, a community garden where amid the herbs, vegetables and flowers are sculptures moved by wind and water, made from found and everyday materials, multicoloured and just great *fun*.*

Listening to Alan Lane, the artistic director of Slung Low, a theatre group based in Leeds, most recently at the oldest working-men's club in England,† here is another great case study for how to enmesh opportunities for creativity in even the most deprived communities. 'DIY culture' might not always look like what the graduates of fine arts think it should, but if people are getting together, making their own entertainment, drawing on their own experiences and (probably, given where we're starting from) mashing that up with samplings from popular culture, great! Community karaoke is much better – healthier – than people sitting in their bedrooms, individually watching Netflix.

There are possibilities in the technologies and capacities now available to almost everyone, at least in the UK. A basic smartphone (which you need anyway to get Universal Credit) is a tool that can make a pretty snazzy video, whipped up with access to free Wi-Fi in the library (if you're lucky enough to still have a library). I am old enough to remember when there was great excitement about the democratic cultural possibilities of 'the internet'. Those have not gone away.

Remember MySpace? It was the first social media

* With sad inevitability, the Green Backyard was threatened with closure in 2014, when the council decided it wanted to sell the former allotment site for development. After a long struggle it is now, I believe and hope, safe.
† Recorded in *The Club on the Edge of Town: A Pandemic Memoir* (Salamander Street, 2022)

platform, bought at vast expense by Rupert Murdoch, now little known. The dominance of Facebook (already fading), Twitter/X (ditto), TikTok and Instagram are not permanent. We can look to shape the regulatory, economic and social framework to ensure something better, more democratic, more open to creativity, less commercial, replaces them. Borrowing the terms of Australian writer McKenzie Wark, that is the hacker class taking over from the vectoralist class* – a democratisation of cyber and real spaces, everyone a creator, having a space in the new world.

Who can be an artist?

But who is going to be exercising their creativity? Without opportunities to develop ideas and skills, and to embed the idea of personal creation, where will not just the future UK stars come from, but the people who will take theatre into schools (when they have the funding for it)? Who will work with a local community to paint a mural, or teach craft skills at the local college? Under current creative-sector policies, we know the answer to that. They will come from the fee-paying schools, where creative subjects continue to be taught as they are slashed from government-funded schools, particularly in poorer areas. They will come from the families with social capital – and the cash to support years of exploration, development, and quite possibly the recording of the first tracks, or the production of the first couple of shows.

---

* The few who control the means by which information is shared, and gathered, in cyberspace.

Mainstream institutions occasionally have panic attacks about the narrow and unrepresentative range of society from which their new talent is drawn, and set up a new scholarship or promise to change recruitment practices, but without starting in kindergarten and continuing through to postgraduate in spreading opportunities for creative growth, that is never going to produce real change. The 'Cool Britannia' so beloved by Tony Blair came from a period of what now looks like remarkable equality of opportunity for all to get involved in the arts – oddly the Thatcher years, with that financial support. We will all be much the poorer for the narrowness of perspective, the lost talents and the lesser creativity if we continue to only allow creative education and development for the privileged few.

There is a further question to be asked about what use the skills we already have are put to. In 2020 Advertising Week, I could not resist participating in a debate titled 'The ad industry has a greater role to play in fighting climate change than politicians'. You can see why they invited me, and I can guess what they expected me to say: that they should all focus on promoting solar panels rather than Coca-Cola. I did point out that collectively they devoted massive resources to trying to convince the public that an oversized, dangerous lump of metal and plastic in the form of an SUV will give us the life of an intrepid explorer, powering over mountains and swishing through rivers, when actually it will be stuck on a fume-choked suburban road, filled with fractious and unhappy children, going nowhere.

But I went considerably more radical than that, suggesting, very respectfully, that the problem was their entire industry, dedicating so much effort, talent and skill to turning people into subjects rather than actors. Would they not rather, I suggested, be using their creativity to help make a world *not* based on selling neatly prepackaged products (even admirable, planet- and people-friendly products and activities) to passive consumers? What that world needs instead is inspiration, ideas, images, creativity, the sort of surprising, exciting, enrapturing, gripping emotions that we get from a great work of art, a wonderful novel, a touching film, a shocking painting.

The future economy

The effective ending of education in music, art, drama and related subjects for all but the privileged will have consequences that even a Conservative government should be able to understand – financial consequences. That is a staple subject for the government press-release machine; they must have the framework saved. Take just one example from January 2022: 'Creative Industries Are "Industries of the Future" Minister Tells CIC Event'. Pre-Covid, the growth rate of the creative sector was four times the overall UK average, ministers never tired of relating, usually while a colleague down the corridor was talking about ending 'low-level' creative university subjects as another talked about focusing schools on 'core subjects'.

The UK does have multiple advantages in the creative sector. The English language is a huge selling point, reaching easily the US and multiple Commonwealth markets, and much of educated Europe, the Indian subcontinent and, increasingly, other parts of the Global South. The leftover impact of empire means most of the world knows a lot more about UK (at least English) history than that of any state but their own. The number of overseas students who have studied here and the massive, unbalanced concentration of global media in London, also have an impact. But taking advantage of that means developing the talents of UK residents. Culture is, slowly, decolonising, the Global South reaching beyond colonial borders – with Bollywood, with K-pop, with Iranian films – and the UK could easily be left behind as a historical curiosity.

Essential for wellbeing

The lack of opportunity to learn to express yourself has life-long consequences, means that we are setting up people to fail to find a place in society, and impoverishing us all by missing out on their contributions. This was driven home to me in 2016 when I visited St Gabriel's High School in Bury, Greater Manchester, to talk to Year 10 and 11 drama students and watch extracts from their exam performances. They were determined to meet with me – logistics meant the visit was only achieved at the second attempt – to express their anger, frustration and disappointment at the government's English Baccalaureate plans. Pushing English, maths and science even harder meant their younger schoolmates would not have the chance to study drama that they had enjoyed.

I was ready to make polite noises about the performances, but I had no need to act: they were brilliant, powerful expressions that would have been excellent from university students.

Talking to the pupils, some wanted to pursue the career possibilities of drama, but for others, this was also a crucial
chance to shine and be valued, when sitting down for a written exam in English or maths just was not their thing. And
all agreed that learning to express your emotions, to find a
way to shape, understand and share them, was useful, often
crucial, for their mental health.

Not just a luxury for the privileged

We tend to think of non-professional art – the adult-
education painting class, the pottery studio, the practice of
crochet or knitting, gardening, even – as pursuits of the middle
class, often retired, often women. Those are the people who
are most likely now to have time to pursue them. The
facilities – reliant almost exclusively now on user pays, without government funding – are concentrated in wealthier
areas. But in a universal-basic-income society, one where, as
we will discuss in the next chapter, the luxury of space is de-
privatised and made accessible to all, everyone would have
the chance to develop their creativity; not, necessarily, as it so
often is now, as a desperate side hustle to make a few extra
pounds, but simply for the pleasure of it.

But there is a problem with skills, and the development of
creative impulses. If you have never – through the education
system or later – had the chance to develop them, it is going
to be hard to know where to start. I once, as a manager, had
to counsel a staff member who was having serious debt problems, which were visibly affecting her work. I sat down to
discuss them – and her shopping habit. Most lunchtimes she

came back with a bag of new clothes, and spent Mondays talking about her weekend shopping expeditions. I asked her what other things she might do in her leisure time. She could not come up with a single suggestion – a product of a society that has educated its young to think that entertainment is something you buy, not something you create or participate in.

Creativity is dangerously democratic

Thailand in the 1990s, watching as the government slowly, reluctantly expanded the education system in poorer areas beyond primary-only, gave me an insight into why many quasi-democratic regimes in the Global South are reluctant to invest in education. Giving voters more knowledge, introducing the idea of critical thinking, providing the confidence to answer back, often does not seem desirable to the status quo in power, even when the economic advantages are obvious.

It is an insight that I have been forced to transfer to Westminster. The desire to make schools into exam factories, to privilege science, technology and engineering subjects over humanities, to make education about ensuring pupils are 'jobs ready' is not just an economic one. Critically examining social structures, seeing how they could be different, painting (literally or figuratively) images of a different world, are not something our current power structures (of either major party) want to encourage. In 2014, I was privileged to take part in an event inspired by the artist Monica Ross, a recitation of the Universal Declaration of Human Rights in the British Library foyer – a very public exhibition of the importance of rights that, even then, were obviously under threat.

Artists and creative people, allowed free rein rather than being corralled into an advertising agency or a game studio, are well equipped to see what is wrong about our current society and create images of how it could be different. I saw a wonderful example of this at the Preston New Road anti-fracking camp, where waste plastic had been woven into a mesh fencing panel, creating a beautiful image of grazing sheep and cattle, green fields, sunshine and a rainbow. It was directly in front of a scene that had been like that, until a giant concrete pad had been laid, a drilling rig installed, and HGVs set to rumbling in and out.

Please hope!

Whenever I talk to creative people, I always get in a semi-serious plea: please, no more apocalypse novels, zombie movies, climate-breakdown plays. Instead, *please* can we have lots more productions that imagine what 'it all works out fine' looks like. Let's have a Hollywood romcom – boy meets boy, boy loses boy, boys get back together and they all live happily ever after, which is set, say, thirty years into the future, with society being genuinely democratic, renewable-powered, with a three-day working week and relocalised economies with great, healthy food and comfortable, afford-able housing. Just as the background.

One of the few examples of this being attempted – and it is still a 'political work' – is Jonathon Porritt's *The World We Made*, set in 2050. Its main character, Alex, is a teacher who works three days a week in that role and two days a week as a volunteer, lives in a solar-powered home, and walks and cycles in their fifteen-minute city. Alex sets his pupils projects to explain how society found its way to one-planet, stable and secure living.* The book is a mixture of those, and the story of Alex's life. But I think Jonathon will forgive me for saying he is not a natural novelist, and there is far more to be achieved in this area.

Manda Scott's Thrutopia project, a self-study course for writers about imagining a better future, is heading in this direction, seeking to creatively work through models for a generative future. The developing genre of solarpunk contains many works along the same lines. Sci-fi veteran Kim Stanley Robinson's *The Ministry for the Future*, described by activist Bill McKibben as 'anti-dystopian', is perhaps the most successful book that could be put under this classification.

---

* In contrast to our share of three planets that we're consuming now. See more at: www.bioregional.com/one-planet-living

Chapter 9
Recovering Space

Housing, sports fields, libraries and streets that were once public have been swallowed into private control, depriving us all of opportunities, of community. Turning a parking place into a playground, a field into a shared garden, a ruined house into a library are projects of renewal that must be open to every community.

What you might call my 'day job' means I spend a lot of time pointing out the failures of ideologically driven privatisation in the UK. Calling for water companies, energy companies, railways and more to be run for public good rather than private profit, taken out of the disastrous private hands in which they have been lodged for decades, is something I probably do in my sleep. It is urgently needed, when the water companies have loaded the unencumbered entities they inherited with massive amounts of debt, most of which has been paid out in dividends to hedge-fund owners based in tax havens, and when unregulated energy companies fall like ninepins, at massive public cost. And the railways – well, the government has now been forced to become the largest rail operator by privatisation disasters, but only reluctantly.[1]

But getting across just how much we have lost with the

neoliberal ideology of the past four decades, which has continued through Tory and Labour governments alike, is a big task. It involves looking further than the obvious privatisations of public services into the land, the houses, the spaces from which we have all been excluded.

Privatisation of housing

One issue on which the Green Party has only just started to win the argument (having always opposed the policy) is Right to Buy, the flagship Thatcher scheme that has seen an average net loss of 24,000 social homes per year since 1991,[2] at least 40 per cent of which have ended up in the hands of private landlords, charging (often the state, through housing benefit) massively higher sums for exactly the same accommodation.[3] That is in addition to, with the discounts on purchases, a loss of £75 billion to the public purse since 1980.

Always an explicitly political project – aiming to turn Labour renters into Tory homeowners – it saw some people win big, with capital gains greatly enriching their at least theoretical worth (although of course this could only be realised when the home was sold). But having lived in three former council homes (buying them from their Right-to-Buy purchasers), I also knew many neighbours for whom this supposed windfall turned into a ball and chain, maintenance and repair costs landing them with unpayable bills that sometimes ended in homelessness. And this was far from atypical – for the 12,000th family to use the scheme, the Pattersons in Romford, Essex, who were visited with much fanfare by Margaret Thatcher, the story ended in family breakdown, to which the financial strain of the mortgage contributed. Maureen Patterson was forced to sell up and move into a caravan.

Accompanying the sell-off has been a failure to build genuinely affordable housing, the combination leading to a great privatisation. It has been a dramatic, but surprisingly little remarked-upon change. In 1979 nearly half of the British population lived in council (public) housing. It was a secure home for life, with affordable rent and some guarantee of living standards, as Lynsey Hanley sets out in the brilliant *Estates: An Intimate History*. (There were council-maintenance failures, but there was hope of political action to fix them.) Yet now that figure for council housing is only 12 per cent, with another 6 per cent in housing-association homes (of varying levels of affordability and public-spiritedness in their operations). We have gone from council housing being for everyone to it being only available for the absolute poorest. Common sense tells us the predictable consequences of concentration of misery and suffering.

It is only in the past few years that the existence of 'poor doors' (different entrances for social tenants and private owners to the same building or complex) has come to public notice, but delivering leaflets around London, it was something I had seen before I heard the term. I think of a block of new social housing in Kentish Town, forced by the planners as a trade-off for a giant private development of flats whose prices soar into the millions. It was built right on a busy road, the worst part of the site, with poky dark corridors whose cheap white paint was predictably scuffed and grubby almost the day the first resident moved in. In many developments we have seen households in such accommodation denied access to facilities – such as children's playgrounds – used by the rest of the private owners and tenants.

What the planning rules could have insisted on, should have insisted on, was 'pepper-potting', scattering the social homes amidst the private, constructed to the same standards. That would be the common-sense alternative. And, of course, building far more council-home developments – on land that councils once owned. The government claims, when I challenge it, to be encouraging alternative forms of housing, new and more innovative forms. But there is little sign of that on the ground. Pioneers have to battle to get schemes started in a system built for the big developers.

Positive alternatives include community-land trusts: communities getting together to develop a site in democratically decided ways, often involving private ownership of homes but where any increase in value is for the good of all, not an individual windfall. Housing co-operatives and co-housing are other, similar routes, enabling flexible, practical housing that meets real needs. I have always loved the idea – although I have not yet managed to visit – of the New Ground Cohousing in Barnet, North London, for women over fifty. This is housing designed from the start as a community facility, tackling issues of loneliness and care provision in a new model that has to be the way forward from the inefficient, isolated, impossibly costly 'luxury apartment' or 'executive home'. People getting together to create the community and homes they need: that is a common-sense solution to the 'housing crisis'.

Public investment, private profit

The sell-off of homes has been matched by a sell-off of public buildings and land that truly deserves to be called a fire sale. Research for the Bureau of Investigative Journalism in 2019 showed that between 2015 to 2018, local councils, struggling desperately to meet even their statutory (i.e., Westminster-directed) responsibilities, sold off £9 billion worth of grand old libraries and town halls, playing fields and sports centres, plus any scrap of land they could find.[4] Brett Christophers in *The New Enclosure: The Appropriation of Public Land in Neoliberal Britain* estimates that 2 million hectares, or 10 per cent of the UK landmass, was sold out of the public sector between 1979 and 2018.

The NHS has sold off wonderful old buildings (and some pretty tatty ones too – but the land below them could have been put to public use). It was a visit to the Isle of Wight, and the former Frank James Hospital, that really helped to crystallise the issues for me. Started as a philanthropic institution, caring for retired seaman, it was obviously, once, a lovely building, in what is known as the Dutch style, by a prominent Victorian architect. It was absorbed into the NHS in 1948 and closed in 2002. During that time it was a local hospital whose facilities and fabric were frequently supported by local fundraising efforts, but when it was sold to a property developer, slated for 'luxury housing' development, the cash went straight into the Treasury. Now it may well be that the building was no longer suited for modern medical facilities, but how is it that the privatisation passed almost without comment, the public contributions over decades unacknowledged?

That the site remains a ruin, subject of continuing legal wrangles, is just one more sign of the sheer wastefulness of the private sector. So many such buildings, supposedly with legal protections for their historical value, have no real security at all. They 'catch fire', are 'accidentally demolished' or are allowed to rot until restoration is 'no longer viable'. (Look up the magnificent Sheffield Old Town Hall if you want to see this process in action.) A long-term community asset is reduced to a building site, on which is often placed an architecturally and functionally dreadful replacement. Looking after what we have, what previous generations bequeathed to us: that is just common sense.

Where can we organise?

One particularly pernicious effect of the sell-off has been to take away what were democratic, crucial spaces where communities got together to organise and act. A case study for this is Caxton Hall in central London. Anyone who wants to run an event around Westminster knows how expensive and difficult it is to secure a space today. Accessible cheap options, such as Caxton Hall once was, have gone. It was built in 1888 as a seat of local government, but with two public halls hosting many key national political events. The alternative Women's Parliament was held there at the beginning of each parliamentary session from 1907, with a subsequent procession to the Houses of Parliament. It was also the site of the Pan-African Congress of 1900, was used for government press conferences during the Second World War, and was where, at the height of the Cold War, in 1955, the

Russell–Einstein Manifesto highlighted the dangers posed by nuclear weapons and called for world leaders to seek peaceful resolutions to international conflict. No hope of such vital use today, however; it has been converted into 'luxury flats' and offices.

The privatisation has not just been of ownership, but of usage, something that is terribly evident in the loss of pubs around the UK. The wonderful Lost Pubs Project (closed-pubs.co.uk) counted by July 2023 more than 42,500 lost pubs. Now, it might be thought that pubs are places of enter-tainment, commercial enterprises, and not to everyone's personal taste, but they are also where different parts of a community come together, meetings can be held, perfor-mances put on (see the last chapter). Often they have been converted to more of those 'luxury flats', and in some poorer areas, simply left to rot. A couple of years ago, visiting Dar-lington, I realised how badly the town, once a massive railway centre, was suffering when I saw empty, abandoned pubs and others open only a couple of days a week.

With municipal facilities closed down, pubs are often the last gathering places left, something that has been recognised by a growing movement for community ownership of pubs. In rural areas they are often reimagined as community hubs – also housing a shop, perhaps a post office, places for play groups and craft clubs. I have visited some wonderful facili-ties like this. But to get such a project off the ground, and keep it running, needs social and financial capital, something that many of the communities that most need the facility lack. In a universal-basic-income society, they could be far more viable, and easier to get off the ground.

Far too many new developments have been allowed to be

built without any such gathering places at all. In Stowmarket in Suffolk, a local Green councillor stood me on the top of a railway bridge and swept his arm across an entire new development that stretched as far as the eye could see. He asked me to guess how many public facilities there were in it. A couple, I hazarded. 'None,' was the answer. They were supposed to be constructed at the end of the project, but somehow it never happened.

Sport and leisure is another area suffering from massive privatisation. Gyms, pools, halls and playing fields have been taken out of council hands and put into private, the fees hiked often well beyond the pockets of local communities. Parks – particularly in the largest cities – are let out for festivals by councils for much of the summer, taking away access to crucial city lungs. There has also been a proliferation of private 'play spaces'. Soft-play centres for younger children are often on industrial estates and in the corner of retail parks, not very visible and also not accessible to parents without the cash to splash out. What had been council-owned adventure playgrounds were often privatised in the early teens of the twenty-first century as austerity bit, and frequently were closed by the end of the decade as models that asked parents to pay many pounds per visit fell apart.

Rebuilding is possible

Putting resources into local communities, giving them the chance to create the indoor spaces they need – as well as the parks and the sporting facilities – is a common-sense way to rebuild. I saw what is possible in the wonderful Granby Four

Streets project in Liverpool, where an area blighted by decades of failed housing policies is being gradually recovered, repaired, and turned into something wonderful by joint community effort. One part of the plan is to ensure that there are community spaces, including a converted former terraced house that is a walk-in greenhouse/winter park. The same might be done in dormitory suburban housing, or in former local shops, as I saw on the Isle of Wight, where I visited a brilliant community project in a disused shop. In Leeds, Latch is a small-scale but exciting project that buys up dilapidated homes and restores them with the help of those who are unemployed, some of whom then get to live in the result.

Social enterprises and co-operatives sometimes manage to pick up the pieces of the privatisation disaster. Sycamore Adventure in Dudley, West Midlands, is a case study where a social enterprise stepped in and now runs a thriving community centre, including a playground that caters to many different groups. But too often such facilities have simply been closed, and handed over to developers for more housing without community facilities.

Rather than creating the problems, then trying to fix them, much better to ensure that all future provision includes community facilities from the start. Preventing the domination of multinational companies, allowing space for small independent business, co-operatives and community facilities, is something many Green councillors have worked on. Think of the classic new block of 'luxury flats' with shopping space on the ground floor. Greens have insisted that space be divided up, so that instead of a Tesco Metro and Sainsbury's Local, it can be a couple of small independent stores, and – hopefully – a community facility as well.

Streets for people

Pocket parks are another initiative that Greens have successfully supported around the country. Even small spaces – sometimes those colonised by the brilliant guerrilla-gardening movement – can become play and leisure spaces for young and old, and everyone should have one within an easy walk of their home. Or, ideally, outside their house, as in Ghent in Belgium, one of many places in continental Europe where a lot of Green ideas have already been put into effect, rethinking the city for the benefit of its people. What is more privatised, after all, than a parking space, a private car, typically stationary for twenty-three hours a day? Usually it is occupying what is ostensibly public land in a city, town or village that could be being put to far better use – as a children's playground, where the young could take their first steps to independence still in view from the family front window, or as a community vegetable garden helping feed the neighbourhood, or simply as a site for a bench, where older citizens could sit and watch the world go by. Instead, for when a car is really needed, it could be hired by the hour – one or two per street instead of a neighbourhood clogged with them.

In Ghent, cars have been effectively expelled from the city centre, and some of the parking spaces put to those uses. It was a Green cabinet member on the city council who pushed that through, against considerable political resistance. Yet I visited just before the next city election, and not one party, not even the far right, suggested going backwards to car-clogged streets. And the Greens doubled their vote in that election.

In the UK, we might not have managed to get that far, but there is a growing, effective 'play streets' movement that aims to shut roads at regular intervals and turn them over to community facilities. I have visited several in action, and seen the giddy excitement of children suddenly granted access to the public space from which they are usually anxiously tugged away by parents. I have seen older people at their gatepost, mug of tea in hand, chatting to other generations on the street with visible pleasure. Why should this only be for special occasions?

An enclosed land

Activist and researcher Guy Shrubsole has been single-handedly responsible for exposing much about the long-term inequity of land ownership, particularly in England, estimating that half of England is owned by less than 1 per cent of the population. That goes back over centuries of enclosures, when forests, grazing land and arable stretches that had been shared by all were snapped up by the aristocracy and gentry, who still own more than 30 per cent of the land area. As I discussed in Chapter 4, the difficulty of securing land for a small farm, co-operative or community garden has huge negative implications for food security – one more blow to public health.

Scotland has seen significant land reform, not going nearly far enough, but certainly steps in the right direction. That is something we also need to see in England. Why should someone own half of several counties just because their great-great-great-etc. grandfather was good mates with

William the Conqueror, or chose sides wisely in the War of the Roses?

Right to roam

Before progess on ownership, there are likely to be advances to access. For growing fast in England is the right-to-roam movement, which is seeking the same access to land as people have had a right to in Scotland since 2003, when a long-existing customary right was codified into law. Norway, Sweden and Estonia have essentially the same rights. That does not mean you can wander up to someone's back windows, or trample their bean crop, or scatter litter into a stream, but it does mean access for responsible use of the countryside. By contrast, in England only 8 per cent of land is available for people – much of it in remote areas like moorlands – and 95 per cent of the rivers are closed off, at least theoretically, to swimmers, kayakers and picnickers.[5] The right-to-roam policy is enthusiastically embraced by the Green Party. When campaigners Nick Hayes and Guy Shrubsole came to the party conference the room was packed with members, including MP Caroline Lucas, who has since put down a private members' bill to deliver the right. The public health benefits – the access to nature, exercise and fresh air it provides for all – are obvious. And the chance for holidays closer to home, no flying necessary.

But the benefits are social as well as individual. The right to roam would open up knowledge of good and ill. The exposure of the illegal killing of raptors, the placing of snares, the existence of dreadful 'stink pits' of the rotting carcasses of trapped and shot animals associated with driven grouse-shooting on our uplands has been made possible largely by public access and recording from land that is already covered under the Countryside and Rights of Way Act of 2000. But the access could also record positive developments – open up huge possibilities for citizen science – popular and growing with everything from the Big Butterfly Watch to long-term British Trust for Ornithology volunteer recording projects. With a four-day, or three-day, working week, there would be time to explore – and with universal basic income, even more possibilities.

The right to roam would also help to expose just how parlous is the state of nature in the UK, one of the worst corners of this battered planet for wild flora and fauna. More than one in seven native species face extinction and more than 40 per cent are in decline.[6] Hedges are flailed to narrow rows of bare sticks, national parks are deserts of rye grass and heather, birds and bees do better in cities than the countryside. More exposure would help understanding, and a drive for change.

I agree with Winston Churchill

This is not a statement I make often, but I agree with Winston Churchill on the subject of land-value tax. The wartime prime minister was in favour of putting a charge on the owners of undeveloped land to reflect its potential value. This position was taken in light of the development of railways and roads, which landowners along the route could benefit from hugely, their land soaring in resale value, while the cost was borne by the public. That argument still applies;

one of the most recent unearned windfalls was in London, along the route of the massively expensive Crossrail development (now the Elizabeth line). But more, it would address land-banking by developers (their aim is profit, not new houses), supermarkets buying up potential sites to keep rivals out of town, and speculators holding inner-city land empty, just waiting for price rises.

Possibly the most dysfunctional, outdated system among the many staggering on in the UK – and boy, is that a tough competition – is the current land-tax system of council tax and business rates. Widely derided and hopelessly regressive, council tax is based on values of 1991 in England and 2003 in Wales because no government wants to be responsible for the uproar a rebalancing to current values would create. It sees owners of homes worth many millions in Chelsea paying little more tax than the residents of modest terraces in the North. That Chelsea owner, who may well also have a home in a US city, is likely to be paying twenty times as much land tax there as in the UK. And business rates see small independent shops shut out of many a high street, while giant Amazon warehouses pay peanuts.

Land-value tax, set at the right level, could lead some landowners to decide that continuing their ownership is not worth the cost. That might set us on the route to restoring public ownership – that supermarket site becoming a new community garden, an inner-city building restored as a community centre. As a long-time resident of Camden in North London, I saw the history of such developments. In the sixties and seventies the council there had been able to buy up much private housing at very low cost and turn it into public housing. There has been a modest return to such schemes with the London Mayor's Right to Buy Back scheme – long promoted by the Green Party – that is returning existing housing to public stock, and even the government has funded a small scheme across the country based on the housing needs of Ukrainian refugees.

Protecting the green belt: not a luxury

Property developers and their friends like to dismiss the green belt as a middle-class obsession, and a protection for house prices. But it is just common sense that compact cities are better cities, where people can gather in public spaces near their home, with facilities – from cafés and laundrettes to greengrocers and games rooms – a short walk for all, and public transport affordable and reliable. Australian-style suburbia, where I grew up, where the highlights of the week were mowing the expansive lawn and washing the car (which you would use any time you left the house), is no way to live. The uses to which the green belt is often put now in the UK is less than ideal: golf courses and pony fields rather than lovely wild patches of forests and healthy allotments and vegetable gardens. But at least what we have got is better than suburban sprawl.

Part D

Shared Resilience

Chapter 10
Repairing the Broken

Societies can no longer the carry the cost of racist, discrimin-atory neoliberal policing, court and prison practices. The Home Office's 'hostile environment' harms all of society. Restoration must replace retribution.

In 2017 I spent a day in Birmingham Prison. It was not because of an anti-fracking protest or a challenge to a government minister, but for the first-ever Debating Matters event, where a group of political figures* debated, then watched, the prisoners debate. It was a fascinating day that left me pondering the waste of human resources that is the British criminal 'justice' system. Some of the inmates were absolutely brilliant, unpolished but acute in their analysis and quick in their rebuttal of the arguments for our societal status quo.

It is little known that Britain has the highest rate of imprisonment of Western European states, and the number of prisoners has doubled since 1993, despite the crime rate

---

* It was quite a mix, including Edwina Currie, twentieth-century Conservative minister, and Vicky Pryce, the economist and former wife of Lib Dem Chris Huhne, who was jailed for perverting the course of justice over a speeding conviction.

going down significantly.[1] At fault for that public ignorance are our two largest political parties, for whom going 'tough on crime' is a reflex that we saw given full play in the May 2023 local elections.

Crime is down, but the average prison sentence is three months longer than a decade ago. Yet nearly half of the people entering prison are sent there for six months or less, even though it is well established that these sentences are far less effective in reducing reoffending than community punishments. The 'lock 'em up' push has made our prisons crowded, dangerous and terribly ineffective at what should be their purpose – rehabilitation. Parts of Birmingham Prison are Victorian, and Dickensian: forbidding, stark walls and tiny windows. And, as a member of staff told me, many of the cells that were built and originally housed one prisoner now held two. Yet your average Briton today is a lot bigger than they were in Victorian times.

Victorian policies in the twenty-first century

It does not have to be this way. Take, for example, the Netherlands, which has a rate of imprisonment half that of the UK, and which has been closing and repurposing prisons over the past few years at the rate of about one a year. That has been attributed to investment in youth-intervention schemes, electronic tagging as an alternative to imprisonment, and residential care for offenders with addictions and mental health problems. That is a summary of the common-sense alternative to our present policies – to acknowledge that many of the people in jail should be getting help, rather than being punished.

The effects of adverse childhood experiences (ACE) on young brains and emotions are well known and yet the criminal justice system fails to acknowledge this reality. More, the economic and social policies being pursued have been multiplying the likely future impacts of ACE. Building more prisons is no answer, but it seems to be the only one our continuing nineteenth-century British political ideologies can come up with.

With the state struggling to keep up with the growth in the prison population, with a degree of sad inevitability, this is one more area – like health – where we have been increasingly following disastrous American models of privatisation. Fifteen per cent of prisoners are now held in private prisons – including institutions set up under the Labour government with the dreadful Private Finance Initiative.[2] They are demonstrably worse than their public equivalents – unsurprising, since profit is being taken out of the funding, rather than being put into staffing, facilities or decent food. But there is an even bigger problem with private prisons: it is obviously in their interest to keep up prisoner numbers, not to cut recidivism by rehabilitating their inmates. In the US they have also been a significant force in promoting carceral policies through political lobbying.

A system made for men

Comments thus far have been about the general prison population, but they apply with even greater force to women prisoners, who are only 5 per cent of the prison population, yet their rate of imprisonment has grown even faster than men's, trebling in the past twenty years, even though there is no evidence for an increase in their level or severity of offending.[3] Women prisoners are quantitatively different from men – far more likely to suffer from addiction and mental health issues, vastly more likely to be victims of domestic and sexual abuse (often associated with their offending) and most wrenchingly of all, far more likely to be lone parents, whose children are then often taken into care. The children are entirely innocent victims of the system.

It would merely be common sense to, as the Green Party wants, greatly reduce the overall prison population, but particularly to end the imprisonment of women in all but the most exceptional circumstances of public safety, following the recommendations of the Corston Report of 2006. It was a stance that saw me take a bit of a pounding in a Reddit 'Ask Me Anything' session in 2015 – the young, mostly male audience finding it hard to understand that women prisoners are indeed a different group of people from males – but I am utterly unapologetic about it. The prison system, the entire criminal justice system, is primarily designed for men, and it does not and cannot cater to this very different and terribly vulnerable population. The rates of self-harm and suicide in women's prisons are heartrending, and magnified by the extensive, long-term lockdowns enforced during the Covid pandemic.

The undeniably innocent prisoners

The 'lock 'em up' policy for people accused or convicted of offences is one horror of UK government policies over decades, through governments of different hues. The locking up, indefinitely, of people seeking asylum – many of whom have been victims of torture and official abuse in the countries they have fled – is a horror on an even greater scale. In the past decade only the Covid pandemic reduced the annual detention figure to below 24,000 (under Labour as well as Coalition and Tory governments).[4] Most people are only detained for a month or two, but in the worst cases their ordeal stretches for years, with no explanation required. The most typical excuse given is that people are about to be forcibly removed from the UK, but in 2020 that was the fate of only a quarter of the detained. The rest are released into the community and the majority will eventually get immigration status of some form.

Campaign groups have carried on a brave struggle to highlight the fate of these refugees, who often suffer great mental health harm (and often physical harm with inadequate healthcare) in detention. In Sheffield, South Yorkshire Migration and Asylum Action Group (SYMAAG) has done great work highlighting issues at the Morton Hall Immigration Removal Centre, isolated in the rural depths of Lincolnshire. But in years of campaigning on this issue, what sticks in my mind most are campaigning visits, led by Women for Refugee Women, to Yarl's Wood in Bedfordshire, which is notoriously run by Serco – immigration detention centres being one more disastrous privatisation. Many of these campaigners were former inmates and visibly affected by the return to a site of what had been torture for them. As we marched along the outside fence, inmates inside opened windows as far as they could to wave and yell their appreciation that they had not been forgotten at this isolated spot.

The common-sense Green alternative is to abolish all routine detention of people seeking asylum, as is the arrangement in many other nations. And even the Johnson government – with Priti Patel driving its hostile environment – funded a trial of alternatives to detention with the charity Action Access, yielding highly positive results, not resulting in less 'compliance' with the system, and saving significant government funds. But scaling up the study into practice looks highly unlikely under either Conservative or Labour parties: what would the *Daily Mail* say?

More, common sense would allow asylum seekers to work, which is, again, the case in many other nations. It has always made little sense to keep people unemployed, in the extreme poverty of a £40-a-week allowance put onto a card, which can only be used in a limited number of shops, for a limited number of goods – and sometimes even seek to prevent them from voluntary work. But now, with the huge labour shortage in the UK, it makes even less sense.

The push to lock up people who have committed no crime (or ship them overseas) has only intensified in recent years, particularly those risking their lives to cross the Channel. The number of people making the crossing has been steadily growing since 2018 as other routes have been closed off. Those intercepted are detained in horrendous conditions and, in some cases, prosecuted and jailed without just cause – as was eventually established by 'activist lawyers' (that is, people working to ensure the law is obeyed). The government forced through, against strong House of Lords resistance, that permanent settlement will be denied to Channel-crossers even when it is unable to deny their refugee status. In quite unprecedented events, the UN refugee agency put out an extensive briefing pointing out all of the ways in which international law and norms were broken by the government's legal changes.

Not Inspector Morse or PC Rowan

If the prison and detention systems are disaster tales for the individuals caught up in them and society as a whole, that is increasingly also true of British policing. For all the rhetoric of 'policing by consent', the paternalism of *Heartbeat* (a television series set in Yorkshire in the sixties) or the faux cerebralism of *Inspector Morse* have never been reflective of the reality of misogynist, racist, classist, often violent and dishonest policing that has been experienced particularly by disadvantaged and stigmatised communities. But the views of the police, and their behaviour, has deteriorated even further over recent decades.

My fellow Green peer Jenny Jones – who has had her own run-ins with the police, having once been arrested (and rapidly 'de-arrested') for supporting peaceful Occupy protesters, and subjected to surveillance for eleven years as a potential 'extremist', while also having oversight of the Met Police as a London Assembly member – has a commendable record of questioning police use of stop-and-search powers. As she has frequently highlighted, young people from minoritised communities, particularly boys and men, have been targeted hugely disproportionately.

We have seen increased militarisation of once almost entirely unarmed police. One of the many concerns I engaged with around the London Olympics in 2012 was that they would provide an excuse for increased use of armed police that would not be reversed after the Games.* And so it has proved. Before the Olympics, you never saw armed police in St Pancras Station. Now they are a fixture. 'Terrorism' will be the knee-jerk response, but as the terrible tragedy of the Manchester Arena bombing of 2017 sadly demonstrated, there are many potential targets. The most effective anti-terrorism efforts need to be directed differently, to focusing on individuals at risk of becoming dangerously detached from society. But that needs to be non-discriminatory and supportive, which is not what we have now.

The Prevent disaster

A great deal of the UK's current anti-terrorism effort comes under the label of 'Prevent', a scheme that aims to divert vulnerable people who might be on the path towards terrorism. The Greens have been leading critics of an approach that has been, rightly, accused of stigmatising and unreasonably targeting minoritised communities, while failing to act adequately on the threat of far-right, fascist and 'incel' communities, particularly online. In 2018 Tendayi Achiume, UN special rapporteur on contemporary forms of racism, racial discrimination, xenophobia and related intolerance, was among the critics, suggesting the whole scheme should

---

* Other major issues included the betrayal of the communities and businesses expelled to make way for the Olympics in a giant, disastrous gentrification push, and the failure to deliver any sustained improvement in access to grassroots sport.

be investigated for its impact on Muslim communities. Compulsory reporting – not part of broadly similar schemes in Norway and the Netherlands – for government officials has been particularly questioned. That has led to many at first glance risible, but nonetheless disturbing, cases of children being victimised.

The dangerous impact of Prevent was brought home to me on a school visit near Leicester, where a brave Year 10 class teacher had enabled her group to discuss the issue and how it was affecting them. They shared their thoughts with me, and I particularly remember the comments of a girl who pointed out that for many of them, the fear of Prevent stopped them asking questions about political, social and international issues, for fear that they or their parents might be targeted. As a sign of how Prevent is pushing underground discussions and thought that would be far better tackled through open discussion and debate – in line with what might be thought of as 'British values' – her comments could not be bettered.

Justice unfunded is justice denied

In the days before the Green Party took over my life, I was aiming – and I will get back to it one day! – to write women's history, which led me deep into history academia, including working with, and writing about, a brilliant digitisation project, the Old Bailey online, which now allows open access to centuries of records from London's criminal court. On its pages are many heart-wrenching stories of injustice and suffering. One that sticks in my mind is that of a woman in her forties and her son, both accused of horse theft. As was true for most of the period covered by the records (1674–1913), they had no legal representation, and faced with the weight of authority and incomprehensible procedures, most had little to say. But this woman begged for her son to be spared, whatever happened to her. The sentence for both, however, was death.

As I campaign – as I often do from my position of vice-chair of the All-Party Parliamentary Group on Legal Aid – for restoration of services that have been slashed into almost non-existence, I think of that little family and their fate. 'Fat-cat lawyers' are an easy target for politicians of all stripes, but no one goes into legal-aid work to get rich. Payments are frequently ludicrously low, and it is particularly difficult for lawyers who come from families that cannot support them as they are getting started, as these are the communities who most need to be served.

Women who need help with family law and protection from violent partners is another area where the slashing of funding has been particularly pernicious. On a visit to Carlisle, I listened to a young woman solicitor talk about the heartbreak of having to tell a female victim of assault by a former partner that there was no legal aid for her to secure a protective injunction when he was released from jail after a term served for assaulting her. It was too long after the assault. The UN Committee on the Elimination of Discrimination Against Women in 2013 expressed special concern about the denial of legal aid to women – another case of the many we have seen over the past decade, of UN officials drawing attention to the failings of British institutions for the most vulnerable.

The figures are reminiscent of the collapse in social housing: in 1949 80 per cent of Britons had access to free or affordable legal help. By 2007 this was 27 per cent, and after the slashing of the legal-aid budget in 2013, the figure is much lower still.[5] The budget for criminal legal aid in 2020–21 in England and Wales was barely a third of what it had been – in pound terms! – in 2005–6.[6]

Courts in desperate straits

As a young journalist in Australia, I saw some of the messes that resulted from unrepresented defendants trying to present their own cases. Similarly in the UK, judges and magistrates – bending over backwards to try to help them navigate the system in the interests of justice – are frequently quoted as noting just how much more pressure this puts on the court system. And this is a system in a state of collapse. The Covid-19 pandemic understandably, and unavoidably, caused a huge backlog of cases, but it is clear the system cannot catch up.

Before the legal-aid cuts, the average length of time for a serious criminal case to go through the courts was around 400 days. It grew to 700 days.[7] For the victims, their families, and for the accused – some of whom, of course, will be innocent – that is two years of torment, of failure to reach a settlement that will allow them to move on with their lives. That is one more disadvantage heaped onto already disadvantaged communities, where crime tends to be most frequent. And a contributing factor is the closure of many local courthouses, with hearings concentrated in larger cities – adding to the costs for all concerned, and the risk of cases collapsing for lack of witnesses. This is one more way in which the state is drawing back into a few large centres – which also has economic impacts for smaller communities.

The Green alternative: restorative justice and crime prevention

Whether it is looking at recidivism rates, the damage being done to individuals in prison or the failure of the system to protect victims, it is clear the current system is utterly failing. The Green, common-sense alternative is to take a different approach. First, we need to acknowledge that the driving factors in crime are social – failures of the education, social care, health and economic systems to provide solutions to problems that end in crime. When right-wing forces – found on both sides of our political fence – call for 'more police', at considerable expense, what might more resources for social care, more funding for teaching assistants, achieve instead? And careful thought is needed – given grave concerns about the culture of police forces, not just the London Met – about whether they belong in some places they are now stationed: schools is one obvious area the Green Party is calling for them to be removed from.

When a crime has been committed, we should focus on the victim, to ask what kind of action will, as much as is possible, restore their circumstances to those before the offence. That starts with the criminal – to ensure that they are making amends as best they can – but also means that society has a role to step in where any amends cannot possibly be enough.

The 'War on Drugs' has failed

Estimates suggest there are around 300,000 regular users of heroin and/or crack in England.[8] That figure alone might be taken as a powerful demonstration that the 'War on Drugs', with its deeply racist roots, has failed. As the charity Drugwise points out, that statistic has sometimes been used as a scare tactic to produce some enormous figures for drug-related crime that do not stack up, but nevertheless, there is no doubt that illegal drugs (and legal drugs – overwhelmingly alcohol) are related to a very large percentage of crime.

Treating problematic drug use as a health issue rather than a criminal-justice one, as the Green Party has long called for, would be the single simplest, cheapest step that could be taken to cut crime rates (together with tackling the enormous scale of legal pushing of alcohol through pervasive and seductive advertising). This common sense is catching on increasingly around the world, including in many states in America, but not in the UK. Portugal was one of the leaders, and it saw drug-death rates, and rates of drug-linked crime, fall, while it has one of the lowest national rates of drug use in Europe.

Dangerous sex-work law

Similar failures are to be found in the classically British chaos of law on sex work. Despite much misapprehension, prostitution itself is not illegal, but many of the practices associated with it, such as soliciting and 'brothel-keeping' are. The latter regulations effectively stop women working together indoors, co-operatively, in safe environments, pushing them into more dangerous conditions.

The overwhelming international evidence is that full decriminalisation of sex work, as has been done in New Zealand, is the common-sense way forward – the way to keep vulnerable women, men and others far safer than the current system. There has been a huge, well-funded campaign for the Scandinavian model – which criminalises clients rather than workers – but this approach simply pushes the industry further underground, into the shadows, meaning greater dangers for the workers.

Targeting freedom

Successive British governments have fuelled the flames of deeply embedded anti-Gypsy and anti-Traveller racism while doing their best to destroy a traditional nomadic way of life by forcing communities into settled homes. In 2021, new policing legislation took the official targeting of Traveller communities to new heights, criminalising trespass and allowing for the seizure of family homes. By removing spaces for travelling families to stop and live, a centuries-old way of life could be ended – discrimination of a most obvious and pointed kind, against a community long targeted around the world, to the depths of genocide.

The same legislation also aims to destroy the right to protest. Explicitly aimed at the Extinction Rebellion (XR) and Black Lives Matter movements, it gives police power to set noise limits, break up 'static protests', impose a start and finish time, and move on solo protesters. It also gives the home secretary the power to determine which acts constitute 'serious disruption', which could lead to demonstrators facing up to ten years in jail.

The Green political approach, by contrast, acknowledges that protest has long been an essential part of winning political advances. The suffragettes are often cited – rightly here – but the practice of what we would today call non-violent direct action goes back a long way, to many documented cases in the English Civil War period. Lady Eleanor Davies, for example, threw 'dirty water' – maybe menstrual blood? – on to the hangings of Lichfield Cathedral in a religious-related protest in 1635.

And Green political thought is grounded in celebrating different ways of life and living: we come back to the principle of diversity being a foundation of a healthy society and environment. We have long stood for the rights and against the demonisation of LGBTIQA+ people, a source of rampant hysteria and hate in large tranches of our public debate today. I am proud that I called a vote in the House of Lords to throw out the deeply discriminatory and disastrous anti-Traveller provisions in the Police Bill, and thank the eight Labour peers who broke their whip for abstention to vote with me (as did the Liberal Democrats en bloc). On some matters of principle it is crucial to take a stand, even when you know you are going to lose.

The joint UKIP/Brexit/Tory/Labour Party line

The government's response to refugees only reflects the way in which the Conservative Party has become the UKIP/Brexit Party in terms of its place on the political spectrum, focused on demonising the 'other' – often benefit recipients, but even more often migrants. But the Labour Party's hands are far from clean in this area. You might remember Gordon Brown coming out with 'British jobs for British workers'.

The first non-conference speech I gave as Green party leader that got any media attention was on migration. Speaking in the Romanian Cultural Institute in 2013, attacking the race to the bottom on immigration rhetoric, I made the same argument that I'd been making on doorsteps around the country to voters who had told me they were concerned about immigration. When I asked them why, typically they said, 'Low wages, crowded schools and hospitals, lack of housing provision.'

I pointed out to them, as I did in the speech, that all of these issues were caused by government policy, not migration – an inadequate minimum wage, inadequately enforced; failure to invest in public facilities or fund local government; and the privatisation of housing under Right to Buy. The media attention for the speech was pleasing, but perhaps not surprising: it was something the media was not hearing from any other opposition source. As I said in the speech: 'The Labour Party has not apologised for taking Britain into the Iraq War, has not apologised for failing to regulate the bankers, has not apologised for the fact that inequality rose in its thirteen years in power – but it has apologised for its immigration policy while in government.'

No champion of human rights

The Conservative Party is by no means one monolithic force. And among the most admirable representatives of it I have seen are Lord Ahmad of Wimbledon, frequently speaking decent words in support of human rights and the rule of law for the Foreign, Commonwealth and Development Office, and a former minister from that department, Baroness Sugg (who to her great credit resigned in protest at the slashing of official development assistance in 2021 but had spoken strongly, particularly for women's rights, internationally). Yet Lord Ahmad is clearly fighting a losing battle on the international stage, for how can the UK push other nations on human rights and the rule of law when it is failing to deliver on the most basic principles within its own borders? As on climate and biodiversity action, the UK is at the centre of media and international focus. When it fails, the whole cause is damaged worldwide.

Meanwhile, government ministers compete to see who can appear in front of the largest Union Jack – a kind of flag-waving nationalism that once seemed entirely foreign to the British character, much more at home in the kind of autocratic regimes we would seem to be lining up against. The teaching of 'British values', as defined by ministers, has been imposed on schools, taking up time that might otherwise be used to encourage political engagement and critical thinking.

Chapter 11

Rebalancing the World

G *lobal minnows can unite to discipline the dangerous,* *superpowers are forced to acknowledge that stability is in their interests too, and the tools for a new international order developed over the past century are deployed.**

Many now see the geopolitical future as uniformly bleak. Lowlights of the current situation include the economically and militarily resurgent China taking a disturbingly Han nationalist path, repressing with genocidal force the Uighur population of its North-East and destroying the 'One Country Two Systems' structure in Hong Kong supposedly guaranteed by the Joint Declaration, following the pattern it had earlier taken in Tibet. There is Vladimir Putin's Russia, still with a massive nuclear arsenal but a hollowed-out, fossil-fuel-dependent economy seeking to restore the Russian Empire with the invasion of Ukraine. Putin has no way to step down, as his arteries keep hardening and the judgement worsening. (Zimbabwe's Robert Mugabe is a parallel that comes to mind.)

---

* An earlier form of Chapter 11 was published in the *Green European Journal*, as 'To Repair its Geopolitics, the West Needs a New Model of Statehood' in 2021: www.greeneuropeanjournal.eu/to-repair-its-geopolitics-the-west-needs-a-new-model-of-statehood

This when the American hegemony is clearly crumbling, economically, militarily and in terms of will. Washington once strode the world proclaiming itself a force for democracy and peace, and – particularly after the Taliban's return in Afghanistan – it is acutely plain that this will not be the case in the future.

Dark history

Before we regard this as an inevitable descent into international anarchy, it is worth looking back, reassessing the actual role of the US since the end of the Second World War. This white-settler empire – built on a foundation of genocide, with a significant element of religious fanaticism and a recent history of slavery, that had engulfed giant former colonies of Spain and France – emerged from the Second World War, having used nuclear weapons as no other nation has, as an unmatched superpower. It had economic and military muscle even two adversaries combined could not match.

There is a story the US still tells itself: that over those decades it kept trying to do good in the world, defending democracy and rights even in the midst of the Cold War. The apparent failure of such efforts is a sign that the Global South just is not developed enough to cope with democracy, according to this account. However, the idea that the West has historically acted or acts now as a champion of democracy around the world is a lazy and plainly wrong assumption that is repeated unchallenged far too often.

Today's world is scarred by the long-term US and UK backing of repressive regimes and leaders, their governments acting in the interests of giant multinational companies that have an iron hold over Western politics. Moral and practical support went to indefensible wars and human-rights abuse. From Thailand, where the monarchy was built up on decades of US and UK support linked to the Vietnam War, to the desperate chaos of Libya and Iraq, where Colonel Gaddafi and Saddam Hussein were 'our men' until they were not, the damaging repercussions of Western involvement are many. It did not start with Afghanistan.

In the Democratic Republic of Congo, a democratic regime at the dawn of independence (1961) was pulled down by US and Belgian decisions, President Patrice Lumumba shot. A Belgian parliamentary inquiry concluded in 2001 that its forces were behind the killing, with US support. In a reminder of the many horrors perpetrated by Belgium on this potentially wealthy nation, Lumumba's body was dissolved in acid, with a Flemish police inspector keeping a tooth as a grisly memento of his nation's action. The tooth was finally returned to his family, and nation, only in 2022. That finally allowed some form of closure on an action that sits like a dark shadow behind all of the subsequent horrors of a nation benighted by continuing violence, often fuelled by the cash of multinational mining companies and manufacturers happy to collect supplies from any source available.

Vincent Bevins' gut-churning *The Jakarta Method* is, in this tale of abusive foreign policy, even higher on the scale of horror, going beyond the destruction of democracy to the mass murder of civilians at US direction. In 1965–6, in the fourth-most-populous nation on the planet, the unarmed, non-violent PKI, a communist party with only loose links to the Soviet Union, much more like the UK Labour Party, was the target of mass extra-judicial killing and an epidemic of torture and abuse. It is estimated that 1 million Indonesians were murdered. This was US foreign policy. The regime of President Suharto was not only vicious, but massively corrupt, his family having amassed by 1998 an estimated $30 billion in assets. Bevins describes how 'a loose network of US-backed anti-communist extermination programs emerged around the world' from 1945 to 1990. He lists the states involved: Argentina, Bolivia, Brazil, Chile, Colombia, East Timor, El Salvador, Guatemala, Honduras, Indonesia, Mexico, Nicaragua, Paraguay, the Philippines, South Korea, Sudan, Taiwan, Thailand, Uruguay, Venezuela and Vietnam. US and UK companies were at the centre of corruption on a similar scale that marked all of them.

The Russians were also doing dreadful things in these years, and the Chinese annexation of Tibet in 1950 was pure imperialism, setting the model for what is now being laid on the rest of non-Han China and Hong Kong. But it was the US claiming to be standing up for democracy – that still claims it stood for democracy and the rule of law. In fact, what most often happened was that the perfectly reasonable ambitions of newly independent nations to act in the interests of their people were identified as 'communism' that had to be repressed, and the interest of US-linked multinational corporations protected.

US and UK policy has not changed in recent years. The dreadful human rights record of 'friend and ally' Saudi Arabia has not prevented massive arms sales. President Trump called Abdel Fattah el-Sisi a 'fantastic guy', in spite of the Egyptian dictator's repression of independent media and civil society voices. The US has backed former Philippine President Rodrigo Duterte's 'War on Drugs' that has involved many thousands of extra-judicial killings, as it once stood squarely behind the hugely corrupt and similarly repressive regime of President Ferdinand Marcos.

Democracy did not have a chance

That most of the world has not succeeded in establishing stable democratic governance and the rule of law – and in so many tragic cases stable governance of any kind – is hardly surprising, when the hegemonic world power was actively, viciously, murderously acting against such an outcome, with the second military power, the USSR, not far behind, and now China playing an increasing role.

Where the US has been successful is in spreading its economic system – and the market for its companies. This is usually called globalisation, but Norwegian historian Odd Arne Westad has suggested, with acuity, it should instead be called 'Americanisation'. The deeply ironic, and sad, reality is that the triumph of that system has produced disastrously high levels of inequality, poverty and hopelessness in the state that drove it, as elsewhere. Real wages in the US for most workers have been stagnant for decades, while the wealth of the richest has soared. Infrastructure built in the post-Second World War boom of redirected military capacity is now falling apart, bridges collapsing, water supplies poisoning whole communities, half the country trapped with snail-like internet speeds. The US is the home of an epidemic of 'deaths of despair', opioid addiction paralleling the wave of alcoholism that followed the collapse of the USSR. One in twenty-five American babies born today will not live to their fortieth birthday.[1]

Many states are at risk of failing in the world today, and the

United States is clearly among their number. I have recently been learning a lot more about the tight enmeshing of the US and UK militaries and military companies, something I want to look into further and explore alternatives. Those who worry about UK 'sovereignty' should really be looking into that.

The dysfunction of a centuries-old, almost-impossible-to-amend, constitution interacts with the need to raise enormous sums from big business and the super-rich for candidates to have any chance of winning elections. The power of incumbency is backed by a tradition of pork-barreling in government spending, where elected representatives direct cash and investment to their constituents over the good of the country. The quality of governance, independent of ideology, is sliding fast. The invasion of the Capitol on 6 January 2021, a mob goaded on by the sitting president, who had lost the election, came as a shock to many. But in the preceding days the Speaker of the House of Representatives had asked the military to stay President Trump's hand should he decide to launch a nuclear war. An assurance was given, but without any real certainty. Asking a relatively junior officer carrying the 'nuclear briefcase' to follow in the brave footsteps of Stanislav Petrov, the Russian who in 1983 refused to follow orders during a false alarm about a US nuclear attack, was a very large ask, and a huge gamble.

A failed US hegemony

We are, as in so many other aspects of life, at a turning point. Maybe what is known as the *longue durée* of history will regard the last seventy years as a slow period of decline of the United States of America, its high point the Second World

War, the rest an account of a flailing, ineffective hegemony, with a huge amount of firepower but little idea how to use it, no consistency in its policy and a long track record of failing to keep its promises. The desperate Afghan people, again in the grip of the Taliban after massive US failures, are the standout victims. It should not be forgotten that the CIA's manoeuvres against Soviet forces in Afghanistan in the 1980s led to the rise of Osama bin Laden.

US military activities have also resulted in massive environmental destruction. Nuclear testing in the Marshall Islands from 1946 to 1962, ironically held as a UN 'trust' territory by the US, led to radiation poisoning, birth defects, high rates of cancer, the 'vaporisation' of at least four islands, and atomic refugees – the people of Bikini Atoll affected twice over, having been returned in 1968 when it was falsely claimed levels of radiation were safe. One mark of the Anthropocene will be the residue of US (and Russian, Chinese, UK and French) nuclear tests. And of course there is also the climate impact of the US military: directly 1 per cent of the ginormous United States contribution, 3 per cent if you include manufacturing for the military.[2]

What next for 'development'?

My thinking about national political development is heavily influenced by what I saw in five years living in Bangkok, and what happened in Thailand subsequently. In the mid-1990s, the royal family was so popular that when the Queen Mother, Princess Sangwal Mahidol, died aged ninety-four, there was not just a compulsory year of mourning in the office in

Government House, in which I was a volunteer, but a second year, decided by the staff. The already ageing King Bhumibol Adulyadej had close ties with the army, but was also presented as a restraint, preventing senior officers getting out of hand. He was a close ally of the US during the Vietnam War, and the BBC played its part in supporting the regime, producing a toe-curlingly sycophantic 'documentary' in 1979 entitled *Soul of a Nation*, narrated by Sir John Gielgud, after the murderous repression of students at Thammasat University on 6 October 1976 led the king to worry about his international reputation.

The unchallenged and unchallengeable place of the monarchy, backed up by an education system founded in what can only be described as brainwashing, meant Thai democracy never really had a chance to get established, the military always in a position to step in whenever its massive commercial interests and political power were challenged. The courts were never able – never even really tried – for any level of independence, the rule of law was not established and today Thailand is a hugely unstable polity, the new king having seized some $40 billion of what had previously been regarded as national assets.[3] Young people are on the streets of Bangkok, now speaking openly against the monarchy, with the potential for bloodshed frighteningly high. It is one more US/UK foreign policy disaster.

For institutions to truly develop, for a functional polity and, hopefully, democracy to arise, internal political forces in a nation have to be allowed to balance each other, to develop mechanisms to deal with each other, to achieve some form of harmony without an outside, overweening force preventing such evolution by putting its weight behind one side. Such a development, of course, is what happened in most of the currently successful states in the world. What develops is a model of organic strength, institutions with strong roots. It is only common sense that will work better than an outside imposition.

Not always a role model

I draw hope from Finland, now seen as one of the most stable and best-governed states in the world. Yet when I visited the Finnish Labour Museum Werstas in its second city, Tampere (which has a lot of similarities to Manchester in industrial history and politics), I learnt about Finland's tragic early twentieth-century history, when the civil war between the Whites and the Reds saw massacres of political, economic and social leaders, of unarmed civilians and surrendered fighters. The horrific photos reminded me of images from the Rwandan genocide.

Yet the relatively tiny country was sufficiently united to hold its own against the great powers of the Russians and the Nazis in the Second World War, and went on to become a much-admired national model. When I was on a study tour on universal basic income there, bureaucrats and politicians had a well-honed response to fangirling ('but we should do so much better'), reflecting how often they host such visits from nations seeking to learn from them.

A century of progress

This is where this chapter turns positive – and looks for common-sense solutions to the current utter mess of international relations. That search starts by acknowledging the significant progress made in the past century, and the ways in which we can learn from bad choices made in the past and take different paths in the future: innovation can, and must, occur in relationships between states and international bodies, as much as within them.

I begin with an agreement unlikely to be familiar to any but the most dedicated international-relations afficionados: the Kellogg-Briand Pact of 1928, also known as the Paris Pact for the city in which it was signed. It outlawed war. Obviously, it did not have the desired effect. And it is most often referred to by those mocking efforts at peacemaking and peacekeeping. Yet I am very taken with the reading of it offered by Yale law professors Oona A. Hathaway and Scott J. Shapiro in *The Internationalists*: that it set out the foundations of an international legal order that meant states could not expect to maintain international legitimacy if they went to war simply because they wanted a neighbouring state's land or resources. Cross-border conflicts between internationally recognised states have declined precipitously over the century, the Russian annexation of Crimea in 2014 being a rare recent exception. Yet even then President Putin felt the need to prepare a smokescreen of pro-Russian demonstrations and install a pro-Russian puppet regime, rather than simply march in. Similarly, he sought justification in false claims about the Ukrainian state in 2022.

The pact paved the way for disagreements resulting often in economic sanctions rather than the drawing of sabres. Yet sanctions are an extraordinarily blunt instrument, directed at an entire people when it is usually a regime that they have not chosen that is the offender against the international order. Foreign policy resulting in – or being able to be blamed for – starving and dying children or collapsed economies is a powerful counter-argument, one that was used in opposition to sanctions against Saddam Hussein's Iraq.

The alternative has come from something civil society has developed, campaigned for, winning increasing implementation of an alternative approach: what are known as Magnitsky-style sanctions, targeted at the individuals responsible for decisions rather than whole societies. Their development follows a common pattern; it is in civil society rather than governments that the bulk of an entire framework of international law has been developed and put, at least theoretically, in place. That starts with the Universal Declaration of Human Rights. It runs through seven major treaties against racial discrimination and torture, and for civil and political rights, economic, social, and cultural rights, women's and children's rights, refugee rights, and the rights of migrant workers. Conventions against chemical weapons, cluster bombs and landmines have limited their use, and civil-society-led work on the international offence of ecocide is well advanced. *All* we need to do in the twenty-first century is implement this framework.

Respected states

How can we head in this direction? There is one group of states where any seriously well-intentioned international geopolitical effort heads. Who do you call when a serious effort at peace development is planned? The 'Scandis'. As practitioners in the field say, 'If you want this to have credibility, you have got to get the Scandinavians involved.'

It is worth thinking about what makes a country truly respected in the world. You might be feared as a military force, or counted as an economic heavyweight, but that is not what makes countries rank as 'good global citizens'. I confess this was something I had not thought about until a few years ago, when in the unlikely setting of the Glastonbury Festival – in the Green talks tent long curated by sadly now gone Green Party stalwart Penny Kemp – I heard Simon Anholt speaking about his Good Country Index. It takes a data-based approach to examining the purely external impacts of each country on the rest of the globe – starting from the assumption that nations have a wider responsibility beyond their own residents, to all of Earth's people, nature and the ecosystems of the planet we all depend on. You can disagree about details of weightings and calculations but, broadly, the Scandinavians are at the top of the pile. The Netherlands and Germany also rank highly.

The Reputation Institute has taken a different approach, taking a representative sample of people from G8 nations. This is less globally focused, more a view of the life offered to citizens but, interestingly, rankings come out more or less the same.[4] Reasons given for rankings can be fascinating; analysts say that desire for effective, well-run government is rising up public priorities, a reflection no doubt of its seeming increasing scarcity.

What about the UK?

Where the UK should be in a common-sense future is what I call, for shorthand, a 'Super Norway'. That would mean using its genuine and practically useful strengths in international affairs for good rather than the destructive force they have been over recent decades of riding on the US's coattails. Those strengths include that the working language of international relations is English (sorry, Paris, not French!), our extensive network of embassies and consulates, and the personal relationships arising from colonial ties, international students and diaspora communities in the UK. It would probably take many decades to begin to be trusted as a truly independent, well-meaning actor, but the time to start is now.

The 'Scandis' are already widely regarded as 'steward states', a concept developed by University of California San Diego law professor Emilie Hafner-Burton. Her very useful book *Making Human Rights a Reality* sets out how the past few decades of international civil society and government effort have developed a comprehensive, normative set of human-rights rules – and entirely failed to deliver them. But the Scandis and other steward states, like Costa Rica and New Zealand, are working at it.

Being a steward state does not mean great sweeping actions but, rather, quiet, patient work, diplomatic endeavours, the funding of civil-society actors, the use of international disapproval as a tool to push for compliance. That means taking human rights seriously, not just using them as a stick to beat those with whom we disagree anyway but against 'friends and allies' as well as rivals, without fear or favour.

It means looking at the evidence of what works in encouraging human rights, the rule of law and democracy, atrocity prevention, plus acknowledging that 'first, do no harm' is a principle that should extend far beyond medicine and deep into international affairs. It means moving hard against corrupt actors in the Global North. Progress has been made, inadequate as it is, in UK, US and EU law in this area. It means reining in the multinational companies who continue their neocolonialist ways. Work towards a global minimum tax rate and against tax-dodging made a significant advance in the UN General Assembly in 2022, against significant US resistance.

More than a superpower story

At the start of 2023, the mainstream journal *Foreign Policy* set out what it thought the 'new Cold War' between the US and China would look like. In short, more dangerous than the twentieth-century one. Which, given how close the world came to disaster then, is something we cannot risk. In the UN Treaty for a Global Ban on Nuclear Weapons (backed by a majority of global states), in the COP climate and biodiversity talks, much of the leadership has not come from the superpowers, but from coalitions of smaller nations, often with some of the smallest at their heads.

If we think back to the last Cold War, there was an

attempt, which did not succeed but had great possibilities, in
the Non-Aligned Movement, to create an alternative force to
the superpowers. Of course China – flinging money around
with its Belt and Road Initiative (trading loans and aid for
influence), and the US – will try to seduce small economically and militarily vulnerable nations into their orbits. But
with economics, with populations, with ideas, the Global
South has momentum, and time, on its side.

No inevitability in history

Common-sense politics means aiming for a world that
looks radically different from today's, one where nations
work together to get rid of nuclear weapons, prevent aggres-
sion and exploitation, tackle the climate emergency and
nature crisis. But it is worth reflecting that where we are
now – with a hideously unstable, weapons-choked, nuclear-
menaced international environment – was not inevitable.
Take the immediate post-Second World War period, when
only the US had nuclear weapons. President Truman was
desperate to see a global sharing of the ownership of nuclear
weapons, for them not to remain only in US hands. Truman
had, in general terms, warned Stalin that the US was about
to unleash a powerful new weapon, but did not provide
details, destroying trust. (Stalin, through espionage, already
knew exactly what the US president was talking about.)
You could run an interesting alternative-history scenario
from that very moment, had the US taken the risk of being
honest.

Different choices could have been made in the past, and

they can be in the future. Ensuring we do not enter a new Cold War is clearly in the self-interest not only of the international small fry who are standout good global citizens now, but of the big players also. To quote former UN Secretary-General Kofi Annan: 'We will not enjoy security without development, we will not enjoy development without security, and we will not enjoy either without respect for human rights.'

Security is the desire of the Chinese, the Russians, the Americans, as much as it is of any other peoples. A common-sense diplomatic approach, what has been described in one framing as a feminist foreign policy, seeks to build on that, to take the international frame of law already in place and deliver the rights it promises for all, pulling down the forces of militarism and exploitation, which the world cannot afford if it is to put the resources, energy and attention needed into the climate and ecological crises, and threats of economic and social collapse.

How to deliver laws

The power of citizens in shaping legal frameworks has been brilliantly evident in the realm of international law, where leadership has very often not come from governments but, rather, campaign groups and committed individuals. Take those Magnitsky-style sanctions. It is a story I was privileged to hear from the originator, Bill Browder, at a meeting of the All-Party Parliamentary Group on Hong Kong. Browder's background makes him an unlikely human-rights global leader. The co-founder of a hedge fund with massive holdings in Russia, he ran afoul of the Putin regime after a massive fraud was directed against his company. A lawyer working for him, Sergei Magnitsky, was targeted, imprisoned, and died with inadequate, and possibly deliberately harmful, medical treatment. Browder's campaigning led to the Magnitsky Act in the US, signed into law by President Obama, allowing for sanctions against individual officials and politicians responsible for human-rights violations. The UK has created, and started to use, similar legislation, as have many other states.

It is an inspiring case of civil society creating a new legal framework, a grassroots-up foreign policy, something we're seeing much more of, most notably with the Stop Ecocide campaign for the inclusion of such an offence in the Rome Statute of the International Criminal Court, driven initially by the late, great barrister Polly Higgins. Such an offence already exists in conditions of war, but the threats are equally grave in the 'peace' of our current economies, which operate as an attack on the natural systems on which all life on Earth depends.

Voice of the people

Such action has a long history, in the run of which I have got to include the women of Greenham Common. Starting forty years ago as a march with little more than a score of determined pioneers, they built a movement that at its peak involved tens of thousands of women, making it the largest women-led campaign since the suffrage movement. Greenham set up many for a lifetime of activism, took huge strides towards alerting the public to the dangers of nuclear escalation, and its denizens were eventually able to watch the missiles depart, taken away under the Intermediate-Range Nuclear Forces Treaty.

I see many of the political descendants of the Greenham women every two years in London, speaking, and acting, against the regular arms fair there. Every fair there are scandals about illegal weapons and sales to abusive regimes. This is one more area on which the fall of Afghanistan is likely to have a large impact: a large part of the $83 billion the US spent on the collapsed military and police forces was for weapons, which appear to have ended up almost entirely in the Taliban's hands.[5] Repressive, vicious regimes fall – they always fall – and if we have been equipping them with a flood of weapons, those will end up in hands unlikely to be friendly to us.

It is a lesson a common-sense alternative will acknowledge, and use as support for the argument that pumping out more weapons into a world already swimming in them is only a recipe for greater insecurity, as well as a huge waste of resources, human and physical, that are urgently needed to tackle our other pressing crises. It is a new update on an old slogan – not swords into ploughshares, rather weapons into wind turbines.

Chapter 12
Making Reparation

The genocidal, extractivist, exploitative mechanism of colo-nialism continues to wreak havoc on this fragile planet and its people. Rethinking the past is crucial for restructuring the present for a sustainable future.

I am an occasional attendee at the London Library history book club.* The subscription being far from cheap, the membership trends old and moneyed, so I find myself in discussions on books about World War Two and nineteenth-century prime ministers, leavened by an occasional dip into the Tudors. When world history comes up, it is usually in a manner broadly sympathetic to the British Empire, which means my views on that – and the whole colonial project – come as something of a shock to other attendees. That is even more true, if less surprising, in the House of Lords, where veteran Tory Lord Cormack, on one typical day, described my account of the Victorian famines in India – where

---

* The London Library is my greatest personal indulgence. A wonderful, private, central-London institution, it was founded in 1841, before state lending libraries, by author Thomas Carlyle, and its first 2,000 books were selected by William Gladstone, John Stuart Mill and Italian revolutionary Giuseppe Mazzini.

millions died as local soldiers, cowed by the suppression of the First Indian War of Independence of 1857, guarded grain shipments out of starving communities – as Marxist. This is one more area where young people's views are frequently at odds with their elders – and I am very much with the Black Lives Matter protesters, the academics counting the cost of colonial destruction of flourishing societies in what is now the Global South, and the economists who continue to point out the neocolonialism of our economic system.

The first time I visited the headquarters of the Foreign Office, it was at a PinkNews awards dinner. There was much to celebrate in the event, but I found it hard to concentrate in the richly overblown setting of marble and gilt. 'Here is where the wealth of India went' kept running through my head. For the Green alternative acknowledges that the world we have now – the wealth of the UK, the US, France, Belgium and other Global North countries – comes from centuries of exploitation.

The genocide that was the Atlantic slave trade, that the white settler colonialism of Australia was another organised genocide, is increasingly officially, if scantily, acknowledged in words. But not in deed; there are no reparations. The shocking fact that the slave owners were compensated, when the empire abolished slavery, with about 5 per cent of the national GDP at the time while the slaves got nothing, is far less known than it should be.

I am proud that the Green Lord Mayor of Bristol, Cleo Lake, removed the portrait of slave trader Edward Colston – before his statue was famously toppled into Bristol Harbour – and put in a portrait by local artist Helen Wilson-Roe of Henrietta Lacks, the Black American who died in

1951 but lives on in a cell line now widely used in medical research, without, for many years, attribution or acknowledgement, or the permission of her family.* But as important as such symbolic acts are as acknowledgement, they are not reparation.

Sometimes, how that might be achieved is quite simple. One case study here is that of the Chagossians – the inhabitants of the Chagos Islands, who as recently as 1973 were thrown out of their homes by the UK to enable the installation of a US military base on their home, a tiny and isolated but strategically significant site 1,000 miles south of the Indian subcontinent. Despite an international court ruling that 'all member states must co-operate with the United Nations to complete the decolonisation of Mauritius', of which it sees the Chagos Islands as a part, the UK has been utterly, and indefensibly, resistant. Most of the actions of colonialism cannot be so neatly reversed as handing back these islands, but in the world of today some of the continuing damage done can be and must be addressed.

Loss and damage

One strand of the COP climate process on which progress has been notably slow is what is known in the jargon as 'loss and damage', on which it was agreed at Paris in 2015 action should be taken (Article 8). But the details were left for later COPs. It is generally agreed that the Global North is

---

* Helen Wilson-Roe also created a sculpture of Lacks that has been installed at Bristol University.

reluctant to acknowledge that the vast bulk of current climate damage – at 1.2°C above pre-industrial levels – is its responsibility, while the bulk of the damage is being suffered in the Global South. It potentially opens the door to massive wealth transfer.

One hundred and thirty nations have got together through the COP process to demand payments, but with the UK in the chair in Glasgow in 2021 no progress was made – although Scotland, as host nation, did put in the first funds of £2 million, a symbolic gesture that unfortunately failed to be matched in any significant way. In 2022 there was a real point of progress: agreement to the principle of establishing a loss-and-damage fund. But the *funding* is yet to be sorted at any scale. As entire nations sink below the waves, as huge coastal areas are lost, fires rage and drought causes societies to crumble, it is in everyone's interests for rich nations to help others adapt to the Anthropocene. It is an investment in everyone's security and everyone's future.

No one is safe

During the height of the Covid-19 pandemic, a crucial phrase became popular, even on unlikely lips: 'No one is safe until everyone is safe.' Usually it was expressed in the context of insincere, undelivered promises about securing vaccines for the Global South. Yet it was not until June 2022 that the so-called TRIPS waiver, a supposed agreement under World Trade Organization rules for access to intellectual property behind the vaccines, was agreed – and was dismissed by campaigners as hopelessly inadequate. Yet already we had seen disastrous new waves of the SARS-CoV-2 virus emerging from the essentially unvaccinated Global South, just as we have seen Ebola escaping from underfunded health systems – and we face multiple similar future threats. As I discussed in Chapter 7, the Green alternative approach is that medical research and production of vaccines and treatments be entirely on a not-for-profit basis, although where traditional knowledge and resources are drawn on, the communities which have developed and held them should receive recompense. Instead, what we see all too often now is Western drug companies swooping in, grabbing the knowledge for free, and pocketing the returns.

True development

I am often challenged, when I talk about UK communities becoming largely self-sufficient in food: 'But what about the jobs and the development in Global South nations if they are not selling us agricultural goods?' It is not a difficult point to answer. If, for example, Kenyans were not growing cut flowers to be flown to UK supermarkets – for extremely low wages, with disastrous exposure to pesticides, and hunger in their own families – they could be producing healthy food for their own communities. If Peruvians were not using irreplaceable 'fossil water', from underground stores that are not being renewed at anything like the pace of use, to provide us with asparagus and avocados, they would be able to try to find a local balance of inputs and outputs while meeting their own needs.

If young women in Sri Lanka, Bangladesh and Cambodia were not crammed into dangerous, exploitative garment factories to produce our fast fashion, they would be available to be teachers and farmers, traders and doctors in their own communities, meeting those places' needs rather than the wants of our multinational companies, at great cost to their own and their communities' wellbeing. There are probably still some fingermarks under a table in a Cambridge college where I had to work very hard to restrain myself while listening to a conventional economist suggest that Cambodian garment workers fainting due to lack of money for food was just a price of 'development'. (In telling this tale, I am often asked, 'Why restrain yourself?' Because yelling and shouting in a debate is no way to win it.)

Despite decades of debunking the idea that 'development' means other nations following in the path of the Global North, and failure after failure by institutions like the World Bank and IMF, the same mistakes keep being made again and again in development assistance. Coffee was a crop introduced to Vietnam in colonial times, and its growth proceeded modestly until the World Bank suddenly thought there was a massive 'development' opportunity, pumping in loans (which of course had to be repaid). But then, since coffee was seen as such an opportunity, global production soared, and the price tanked. Meanwhile, a massive amount of soil erosion and destruction of biodiversity had accompanied the clearing of land, and small farmers were left in the wreckage.

Fair, beneficial trade, not just more trade

Lord Grimstone of Boscobel, former Barclays Bank chairman and one of the many people brought into the House of

Lords to be a minister for Boris Johnson, said, in his maiden speech on the Trade Bill he no doubt thought uncontroversial: 'Globalisation, trade and investment are the best route to prosperity and peace.' He got support from most of the house. For the Liberal Democrats, Baroness Kramer said that 'free, open and fair trade is a bedrock of our political movement'.

Yet there is a problem with that trio. Fair trade is not compatible with the first two labels. How can a smallholder coffee-grower in Vietnam or Kenya really set up a fair-trade relationship with Starbucks or Tesco? Sure, there are organisations and campaigns aiming to achieve that – and I buy fair-trade produce whenever I can, as a better alternative than non-fair-trade – but it is enclosed within the current system, where prices are overwhelmingly set by the global market, and inequality means there can be no real balance in the relationship.

New colonialism in agriculture

Money talks, so the saying goes, and what it is saying is very clear in what is known as transnational land agreements. This means wealthy parts of the world taking control over the most basic resource of all: land, particularly in Africa, from people who are effectively powerless to resist. Typically, traditional small landowners and even those with 'modern' land titles recorded in black and white get little or no compensation when the bulldozers and tractors roll in, and no say in what is happening to them. A few jobs are no recompense to a local community whose life is torn apart.

In total about 32 million hectares, an area the size of Portugal, has been seized in such landgrabs. A study from the Wilson Center in 2008 found that Saudi Arabia, Qatar, Kuwait and Abu Dhabi controlled more than 7.6 million cultivated hectares overseas – funded, of course, chiefly by Global North oil and gas purchases.[1] With food security becoming an increasing global issue, when these farms do actually produce food – all too often it is for biofuels, or simply landbanking for the future – it can only be by force that it will be taken from hungry local communities and shipped to far-off lands. This is human-rights abuse and relies generally on foreign funding for the authoritarianism regimes that enforce the dispossession.

Sometimes it is not land that is being stolen by the new colonialists, but rather ideas imposed. Work in Africa by the Bill and Melinda Gates Foundation – particularly through the Cornell Alliance for Science – is a classic case study. It has worked to promote GM seeds and industrial farming methods, while actively attacking agroecological approaches. It has, however, encountered staunch resistance, particularly from the Alliance for Food Sovereignty in Africa, which promotes small-scale, environmentally sensitive methods using indigenous knowledge and inputs and cutting-edge science to increase the variety, nutritive value and quantity of food available to local communities. Funders such as the World Bank and IMF continue to be instrumental in seeking to impose the Gates approach on communities. How else will they pay back the loans if they are not exporting the products?

What right do we have to rely on other people's soil, water and labour to feed ourselves? Sure, if they produce something extra-special, tasty and attractive, such as spices or coffee, or bananas that cannot be grown at home, there is nothing wrong with swapping that for something we produce that they want, but we should not be taking essential staple foods or nutrients out of the mouths of others, particularly the world's poor, or supporting their lands being taken for cash-cropping to pay back the loans we have given them.

Relying on the market for food has left us, since the 1990s, when most of these figures began to be counted, with a world in which a minimum of 750 million people are regularly going to bed hungry. We have never done better – not really the right word – than that. That is a failed model.

New colonialism in mining

It is impossible to mine metals or other materials without damage – this is a statement of the obvious, but one all too often ignored. The environmental and social costs of mining can be reduced, managed, ameliorated, repaired after the fact, perhaps – but the damage to the fabric of the planet, to the ecosystems on it, to the people who live around a site, those on transport routes from it, to every human being in the use of energy, are all unavoidable. At an event for the Green Economics Institute in 2021, Dr Enkhbayar Shagdar was reflecting on the massive damage done by mining in her native Mongolia, but also the people of Mongolia's need for many of the products of mining, their level of access to the basics of life still being far below what is needed for a decent life.

So what I put forward was a need for 'thoughtful mining':

mining that not just minimises its impacts, but maximises its positive impacts on the human and natural world. Materials extracted to aid the education of girls in the Global South, to extend telecoms infrastructure to them and provide individual internet access there, are very different in their impact to materials used to produce smart toasters and much similar frippery, let alone single-use items. Do we really need 'smart toasters'?

Green alternatives

At COP and other international meetings, there is one organisation's speakers I always try to catch. That is La Via Campesina, a global peasant movement that seeks to empower its own members to take control in their own businesses, their own communities, and to work towards a global model where they get a fair return for their labour. They focus not just on the damage done by industrial agriculture, but the existence of alternatives, all kinds of sophisticated local technologies, many of which still persist, at least in isolated corners, and can be restored, or recovered and recreated. One example: a traditional practice in Niger known as *tassa*. Farmers dig small pits uniformly across fields to collect rainwater and place manure in the bottom of each pit to increase soil fertility. Seeds are then planted in the long ridges of each pit. Particularly in dry years, yields are massively increased.

Many of the organic and permaculture principles that inform some Global North farming have their origins in the Global South. In 1911, in a book honestly titled *Farmers of Forty Centuries*, Franklin King, who had visited China, Japan and Korea, showed that their organic manuring methods produced better results than the artificial fertilisers then being introduced at home. At the Institute of Plant Industry in India, the Indore Process, which involves mixing vegetable and animal waste with chalk, limestone, wood ash, earth or slaked lime, informed the development of the Soil Association in the UK.

Acknowledging that population is not the problem

Some of my frustrating, horrifying political interactions have been with the UK-based group Population Matters. There are some members of it with good intentions, but the typical spokesperson I have encountered fits perfectly the description of a middle-aged white man saying Brown and Black women should not have babies – horrifying paternalistic neocolonialism. But at many of the public meetings I attend, someone will ask the 'population question'. Sometimes it is a global question, often it's an anti-migration 'too many people in Britain' question. And I will internally groan, and go into a response I have made so often that I have to focus on not sounding like a recording.

The human ecological footprint is a product of the number of people multiplied by their consumption, their impact on the planet, yet as discussed earlier in the UK we are currently collectively using our share of three planets. We all have to get to one-planet living, fast. You could halve the UK population and we still would not be at one-planet living under our current systems. Consumption is the problem, not people. To get a sense of what one-planet living might look like, Costa Rica – which tops the Wellbeing Economy Happy Planet Index with excellent health and wellbeing scores at about 1.5 planet consumption – is heading in the right direction.[2]

I have to add that as a feminist of course I am greatly concerned with women having access to contraception and abortion, control over their own bodies, and economic and educational opportunities. All of those changes we know reduce the birth rate. But that is not the reason for doing them. They do not need justification.

Reproductive rights are crucial to a fair, just society. One in six people in the world are affected by infertility – and treatment for that should be available to all, something that feminists from minoritised communities are right to say has not always been sufficiently acknowledged by the feminist movement overall. Everyone should have access to the resources to care well for their children. The hideous history of coercive attempts to control reproduction – from forced abortions under China's one-child policy to forced sterilisation of indigenous women in the Americas, Australia and beyond – should be warning enough that no state should be trying to control reproduction.

Recapturing history

In 2022, the president of the American Historical Association, Professor James Sweet of the University of Wisconsin, wrote a quite astonishing article, being both tone deaf and factually way off-beam, suggesting his discipline was falling into 'presentism' by seeing history 'through the prism of contemporary social justice issues – race, gender, sexuality, nationalism, capitalism', while minimising 'the values and mores of people in their own times'.[3] That assumes that those issues were not front, present and centre in the past. But there were always people fighting against colonialism and extractivism in the societies responsible and in societies subjected to them, even if those people's struggles are seldom found in traditional historical narratives.

When I take visitors around the House of Lords, I always stop in the sumptuous royal gallery at the terrible Victorian fresco commemorating the Battle of Trafalgar. I invite visitors to look at it closely, to try to find the quarter of the British Navy that was then drawn from minoritised communities. (A Black cook was such a Navy standard that it was then the topic of regular (racist) jokes.) Re-presenting history means restoring minoritised people into the centre of the picture. I was delighted on a visit to Manchester to have a chance to see an exhibition on winners of the Victoria Cross and other major military awards who originated from the Indian Subcontinent. One in every six people fighting under British command on the Western Front was from the Indian subcontinent and from 1914–18 nearly 1.5 million Indians served. Rediscovering, studying and teaching such facts is correcting the extremely faulty history with which we are so often presented.[4]

Knowing that there have, throughout the centuries that established our current system, been voices of resistance – at home and abroad – is a crucial support for those saying another world is possible. Had these campaigners been victorious, we would have a different past and present. History is not pre-written, but made. And even though these voices were usually from 'below' – from communities suffering poverty, discrimination and oppression – they made themselves heard, and can usually be recovered.

Chartist leader Ernest Jones, responding to India's First War of Independence in 1857 (commonly called the Indian Mutiny), wrote that *The Times* in its coverage was acting as the 'unprincipled' organ of the 'Leadenhall Moneymongers' for failing to acknowledge that this was a national insurrection. He acknowledged what we would now call human-rights abuses on both sides, but said: 'If they massacre us, we taught them how.' During the 'Jamaica Affair' of 1865, when freed slaves sought to assert their rights to independent lives, rather than being forced to remain on plantations, the abusive and dishonest British governor Edward John Eyre was burnt in effigy by a working-class (largely white) crowd on Clerkenwell Green. John Stuart Mill demanded his prosecution.[5]

What's our place in the world?

There is a persistent historical narrative that sees the UK often compared with France, and held out as having done much better in acknowledging and accepting the damage it did as a colonial power. That is utterly false. How the UK came to terms with decolonialisation is telling: a concocted claim that the idea of colonialism was always to 'help up' the colonised, to get the peoples conquered to a 'fit condition' to govern themselves. But it helped the UK come to terms with the loss of (most of) its empire.

In finding a new place in the world in the immediate postwar period, the so-called 'Special Relationship' with the United States of America was key. After the Iraq and Afghan wars, that came into question – and the arrival of President Trump made it look even more fragile and unwise. In parallel, of course, was our relationship with, and membership of, the European Union, forming an English-language bridge into it. With that position now destroyed by the Brexit referendum, the UK looks, and acts, lost. Evidence is clear in the government's obsession with claiming to be 'world-leading' in every field under the sun, a classic gesture of insecurity.

It is also evident in Britain's continued ownership of about 1 per cent of the world's nuclear weapons. The cost is immense; replacement of our current submarine-launched Trident missiles (one submarine is always at sea with missiles on board and ready to launch) is estimated at more than £200 billion.[6] Whether the UK actually has the independent power to use them is doubtful, but even ignoring that, I invite audiences to consider, as individuals, whether they would use them. Imagine you are the prime minister and you have been told, incontrovertibly, without any chance of a mistake, that nuclear weapons have been fired at, and will land in, the UK. There is no way of stopping those incoming missiles (something I find many do not understand; nuclear missiles do not duel in the sky like Battle of Britain pilots). Will you press the button, kill tens or hundreds of thousands of innocent people in response, when it will do nothing to help your own people?

Truly world-changing leadership

I set out in Chapter 11 how the UK could shape up as a 'Super Norway' in leading the world. Trust would not come quickly or easily, but there are foundations to build on. And one way of doing that would be to become the first nuclear power to sign up to the UN Treaty on the Prohibition of Nuclear Weapons. That has come a long way since the International Campaign to Abolish Nuclear Weapons (ICAN) won the Nobel Peace Prize in 2017. The treaty is now in force, with the backing of 122 countries. But not any of the declared (or known but undeclared) nuclear powers. Here is a genuine chance for the UK to be world-leading.

I have talked about the need for social innovation, and this is probably, with universal basic income, the key proposed change in this book. Science gave us 'the Bomb', but social innovation has yet to stop it threatening our very existence, to deliver the certainty of safety to non-combatants Abbot Adomnán was seeking a millennia ago. Some nations are trying to prepare for nuclear war, with a commendable desire to protect their people; Finland, South Korea and Singapore are among the states with a network of nuclear shelters. But as the Red Cross says: 'No nation is prepared to deal with humanitarian catastrophe generated by a nuclear detonation. No international body could address, in an appropriate manner, the immediate humanitarian emergency nor the long-term consequences.'

I refer to the nuclear-ban treaty regularly on social media, and get a standard set of kickbacks. First, that nations could keep, regenerate or develop weapons even after a ban came into force. Well, the nuclear powers have developed very effective methods of keeping watch on what each other is doing, and the idea is not to trust in disarmament, but verify every step of the way, and keep a very close watch thereafter. Second, that others might not follow. There are no guarantees, but with the huge challenges facing China, Russia and the US – massive environmental threats and ageing, reducing populations – freeing their people from the cost of renewing the nuclear arms race and ensuring they do not risk global destruction are powerful potential motivating forces, if someone will just lead the way.

This subject belongs in a chapter on colonialism because what could be a greater abuse of national/imperial power than being one of a handful of states threatening to destroy the planet and the lives of billions? Should the worst happen and we have a global nuclear conflict, when, millions of years hence, the planet recovers and some new species develops archaeology – maybe the dolphins – they would surely see it that way. And wonder that a species with as many capacities as *Homo sapiens* could have been so monumentally stupid as to create, maintain and use weapons to destroy its home beyond any hope of survival.

Conclusion

Greenism: A Complete Political Philosophy

I am not sure whether to most blame Plato or Hegel for the idea that reasoning is best done by lining up two opposing arguments and fighting it out between them. It is not the complete foundation of the idea dominant for the past century that nations have a choice between two poles, but it is certainly a contributor. So, 'Do you want socialism or capitalism?' has been seen as the central political question. (Or for the UK and the US, in terms of the largest parties, 'Which form of capitalism?') The hope that the human race can move on to something different, and better, has been squashed. I hope it is now clear to the reader that there are, must be, other ways of organising our societies and economies.

This book is an expression of Green philosophy, a working-through of what a unique, complete system could deliver: a vision. I was often asked, as Green Party leader, 'Are you a socialist?' Or accused of being a 'watermelon Green': red on the inside, green on the outside. At times the fruit analogies went wild: mango greens, spinach greens – quite enough for the weirdest smoothie. My answer was always 'No, I am a Green.' That philosophy contains a large amount of thinking that might be classed as 'socialist' – which is not unique to me, but can be found in the programmes of most Green parties across the globe. As the philosophical basis of the Green Party of England and Wales says, 'economic and environmental justice are indivisible'. Virtually all Green parties around the world are on the left of the political spectrum in traditional framing. But Green political philosophy goes much further from the status quo than socialism. It is built around the realities of the twenty-first century, not the nineteenth.

Why is social justice Green?

There can be no such thing as a coherent right-wing Green political philosophy. (Which is not to say that some people do not claim such, but being in favour of conserving species or ecosystems without understanding the underlying causes of their destruction is conservationism, not a political ideology.) In the UK we are using our share of the resources of three planets every year. We have to get back to one-planet living, fast, but if the direction was 'everyone cut back by two-thirds', that would leave a lot of people dead: the people already switching off the heating in winter and shivering because they cannot afford the bill; the people skipping meals now so their kids can eat.

So the people currently consuming a lot, the rich, have to consume a great deal less. Many people now need access to more resources and, particularly, secure access to those resources: certainty that they will be able to put food on the table and keep a roof over their head. That is true in the UK; when the scale is global, it is massively more true. There are enough resources on this planet for everyone to have a decent life, for the climate and nature to be restored, if we just share them out fairly.

Co-creating the world

Green politics also has a different vision of what political leadership looks like. Coming out of Victorian times, the older political philosophies have never shifted away from the 'Great Man' theory. The leader determines the direction, the image, and a party stands or falls on the shoulders of one person. That is really bad, practically: everyone makes mistakes, is human, has flaws in their character, and as Jacinda Ardern recently had the courage to admit, gets tired. And it is really bad for the quality of decision-making – one person's brainwave written on the back of an envelope and then turned into a *Times* headline as a government policy announcement (the way much policy is made in Westminster) is no way to run a country. A group of people sitting down, carefully considering the evidence, the goals and the means, and drawing up a plan – now that is a form of governance to get behind*.

One of the main messages I have co-created with many others over the past decade is that politics should be what you do, not have done to you. And everyone can do politics. I am not chiefly referring to voting in elections, standing in them, campaigning in them. I mean organising a litter-pick, starting a campaign for a pedestrian crossing so the kids can

---

* These are issues I explored with Edouard Gaudot in a series of articles for the Green European Journal: www.greeneuropeanjournal.eu/focus/no-knights-no-saviours-leadership-in-crisis/

get to the park safely, school classmates getting together to demand change in their curriculum. Or making a TikTok video, or starting a petition. ('Clicktivism' is too often demeaned. It is politics, an essential, if not sufficient, driver of change.)

'Take back control' was the sentiment that won the 2016 Brexit referendum for Leave, but behind it was a message that you are powerless, and you need someone – a celebrity leader, be it Jeremy Corbyn or Nigel Farage – to ride to your rescue. The Green message is different – it says 'You can make a difference.' We will help, we will support, but it is up to you to choose both the direction and provide the propulsion.

Years ago I visited a middle school in the Midlands, with pupils up to age fifteen. It was a Catholic school, in many ways very conservative; the school council had just won the right for the girls to wear trousers. When they told me that, I resisted the urge as a feminist to thump my head on the table and wonder what century we were in. But I did not, for the school-council members were cock-a-hoop, riding high on their victory, and, empowered, were looking around for their next target. They had decided on winning the right to use their phones at lunchtime. I was not so sure about that as a priority – but it was their collective decision, their direction.

A truly democratic world, with local decision-making feeding upwards to new global patterns, the setting for that Hollywood romcom I imagine set thirty years in the future will not look exactly like I, or the Green Party, imagines today. And that is fine. But the product of the energy, time and talents of billions of humans, working with respect for and in co-operation with all of the living creatures on this planet and the immensely complex ecosystems on which they and we depend, can be a truly caring, humane, just world. We do not have to repeat the 1930s and 1940s. It is our choice to seize the democratic power to stop it happening, to turn away from that far-right leader shouting crude insults at anyone they determine an enemy of 'the people'. We can jointly choose a positive direction, rethink the ways our societies operate, restore that which has been frayed and worn down, rebuild anew a sustainable, caring, joyful way of living.

Acknowledgements

My mother, Joy Louise Bennett, was emerging as an adult in 1966, the year of my birth, in what one author has judged to be the worst possible year to be a woman in the West.* She was damaged but magnificent, utterly lacking in confidence in her own abilities, with little education or training, but determined on one thing: she would make a contribution to me and to the world without demanding payment in return. As a teenage rebel against her mother, my grandmother, who controlled the first decade of my life, I was not always kind in demanding that my mother rebel with me. Mum gave me that immensely precious gift of unconditional love, while my grandmother, unintentionally, prepared me well for my professional life as a journalist and a politician. I learnt from her, the hard way, that you should never believe what you are told unless you can confirm it from an independent source. Mum's death in a car crash in 1989 taught me something I always hope others do not have to learn – to ask, any time that things go wrong in your life, is it as bad as that moment? It never is.

---

* *How Was It For You? Women, Sex, Love and Power in the 1960s* by Virginia Nicholson.

My partner when I was leader of the Green Party, Jim Jepps, who was also my campaign manager in 2012, taught me a lot about politics, and was a strong support in the tough times. I greatly regret that his becoming a victim of the vicious, unjust, personalised attacks typical of British politics was one price of the Green Surge of 2015. And in those tough times of 2015, I have to pay credit to then London Assembly member Darren Johnson, who held me together when I was, for only the second time in my life, in danger of falling apart.

I cannot name them all, but many, many Green Party colleagues and staff, in the past and continuing, have played a big part in shaping the thoughts in this book. They are all leaders – and as is always true of fast-growing political movements, they carry an enormous load, often far too much. 'Look after yourselves,' I say, while acknowledging that at the same time I am often also asking for more from them. I hope this book will bring many more into the Green family to make your lives easier.

Further Reading

Not all of these books are direct sources for *Change Everything*. They offer routes into deeper, different thinking, both about the past and the future. It is a personal selection, not a textbook one. Lots of other books are mentioned in the preceding chapters. I have not relisted them all.

General

Doughnut Economics by Kate Raworth
If you read one book to understand what our economy needs to do, this is it. Kate also has a very accessible website: www.kateraworth.com

Post Growth: Life After Capitalism by Tim Jackson
A mainstream economist by training, Tim has been on a journey from *Prosperity Without Growth*, which started as a report for the Blair government and set out clearly how you can reduce the carbon intensity of GDP growth, but not decouple them.

The Spirit Level: Why More Equal Societies Almost Always Do Better by Kate Pickett and Richard Wilkinson
A classic: two health economists show, with a multitude of figures and graphs, how even the rich are worse off in more unequal societies.

Here on Earth: A New Beginning by Tim Flannery
Australia's foremost public intellectual, and former head of the Climate Commission, blends examination of non-human and human nature, and ideas, to offer hope.

Chapter 1: Decommodifying Time

The Case for Universal Basic Income by Louise Haagh
An accessible, informative introduction, written by the former chair of the Basic Income Earth Network, the international organisation for UBI.

The Dawn of Everything: A New History of Humanity by David Graeber and David Wengrow
A wonderful exploration of just what human creativity has been capable of over 100,000 years and more. Reminds us just how narrow and limited today's society is.

The Case for a Four Day Week by Aidan Harper, Alfie Stirling and Anna Coote
A manifesto for a campaign fast being put into effect, it is a little prescriptive in its title – the three-day week that the New Economics Foundation was exploring a few years ago is my aim – but this is a book setting out action already being implemented now.

Chapter 2: Education For All, For Free, For Life

School Wars: The Battle for Britian's Education by Melissa Benn
Written more than a decade ago, this is now both description and prophecy – of how a system built on competition, focused on exams, and heavily influenced by business interests, is failing our children.

Universities Under Fire: Hostile Discourses and Integrity Deficits in Higher Education by Steven Jones
A professor of higher education at Manchester University explains the forced marketisation of universities, and the need to restore them as collaborative communities of scholars at all stages of their development.

Herodotus in the Anthropocene by Joel Alden Schlosser
What can academia do for us? Rediscover and reformulate our understanding of the past and apply it to the present. Schlosser is clearly a fan of the Father of History, and makes a real case for rereading him.

Chapter 3: DIY Politics

Nation of Devils: Democratic Leadership and the Problem of Obedience by Stein Ringen
One of the books I reference most often. It demonstrates that majoritarian political systems, like those of the UK and US, produce a far worse quality of governance, irrespective of ideology, than proportional ones.

The Social Instinct: What Nature Can Teach Us About Working Together by Nichola Raihani
The human animal evolved using the building blocks of every species that came before us. Nichola provides many examples of the case I often make, that if we'd been 'by nature' selfish, our species would never have survived. And nor would many other species.

White Freedom: The Racial History of an Idea by Tyler Stovall
Still-dominant Western ideas of freedom developed in a period of slavery, industrial misery and racist ideology. We could learn from

children and pirates about how to find genuine 'savage' freedom. Academic in structure but hugely important.

Chapter 4: Restoring the Earth

Food (Resources) by Jennifer Clapp
Our food system, as so much else, has been financialised, and put into the hands of a few. Competition? There is a show of it, but no reality.

Miraculous Abundance: One Quarter Acre, Two French Farmers, and Enough Food to Feed the World by Perrine and Charles Hervé-Gruyer
How do we eat healthily and sustainably? This is not the complete answer, but a big part of it.

Entangled Life: How Fungi Make Our Worlds, Change Our Minds and Shape Our Futures by Merlin Sheldrake
Wonderfully readable; an exploration of the amazing complexity of the systems we are only just beginning to understand and that we must work with.

The Probiotic Planet: Using Life to Manage Life by Jaimie Lorimer
Bringing together microbiology, immunology, ecology, Earth Systems science, sociology, philosophy and conservation biology, Lorimer's work is founded in the understanding that symbiosis (co-operation) is the key to maintaining life and stability, as Lynn Margulis understood well before the genetic analyses proved her right.

Chapter 5: The People's Economy

Who Cooked Adam Smith's Dinner? A Story of Women and Economics by Katrine Marçal

As a judge I did not vote for this for the 2015 Bread and Roses Award (sorry!), but it is a brilliant, highly readable exploration of the understandings of feminist economics. And an excoriating demolition of mainstream economics.

Plastic Unlimited: How Corporations Are Fuelling the Ecological Crisis and What We Can Do About It by Alice Mah
In the depths of the pandemic, I gave an online talk for Speakers for Schools about plastics, and the invention by Coca-Cola and others of the term 'litter bug', blaming the individual for the problem. This is a detailed, powerful account of the corporate push to keep fossil fuels in our lives through plastics.

The Song of the Shirt: The High Price of Cheap Garments from Blackburn to Bangladesh by Jeremy Seabrook
Another book I did not vote to give the 2015 prize to, but a highly readable explanation of the unbearable human and environmental cost of fast fashion.

Chapter 6: Controlling the Money

Treasure Islands: Tax Havens and the Men Who Stole the World by Nicholas Shaxson
The book that taught me about the City of London, and the long-term and continuing dominance of its financiers. Sets out the shape of what the Panama Papers and so many other leaks since have made crystal clear.

Debt and Austerity: Implications of the Financial Crisis, edited by Jodi Gardner, Mia Gray and Katharina Moser
Making the poor, the disadvantaged and the young pay for the greed of the bankers – that is the story of the past decade, and this

collection of papers is horrifying in its account of some of the human costs.

The World for Sale: Money, Power and the Traders Who Barter the Earth's Resources by Jack Farchy and Javier Blas
In 2006 the multinational trading company Trafigura was responsible for the dumping of 540,000 litres of toxic waste in Ivory Coast. After the 2014 Russian invasion of Ukraine, another similar firm, Glencore, was a major player in stopping the Russian economy collapsing. Only now, with concern about oligarchs and dictators growing, is the story behind this being told, by brave writers and publishers taking on the injunctions.

Chapter 7: Enabling Wellbeing

Health is Made at Home, Hospitals are for Repairs: Building a Healthy and Health-Creating Society by Nigel Crisp
Does exactly what it says on the tin. A practical exposition that sets out the case for putting public health at the centre of government decision-making.

Recovery: The Lost Art of Convalescence by Dr Gavin Francis
Widely, glowingly reviewed, this little book reminds us that we are biological beings, that cell repair and muscle restoration take time, space and peace. Something available to the few now.

Losing Eden: Why Our Minds Need the Wild by Lucy Jones
Contact with nature is crucial for our mental and physical health. Grounded firmly in peer-reviewed science, rich in stats, yet highly readable and memorable. Why do children now spend less time outside than prisoners?

Inflamed: Deep Medicine and the Anatomy of Injustice by Rupa Marya and Raj Patel

Disease is rooted in inequalities of power. The rates of death and suffering in ethnic minority communities from Covid-19 are not an accident. Read it and weep. And get angry.

Chapter 8: Unleashing Culture

Sand Talk: How Indigenous Thinking Can Save the World by Tyson Yunkaporta

In the UK, we're struggling to implement systems thinking, to get beyond siloed academia and government. Yunkaporta demonstrates that joined-up thinking – a consistent, coherent way of understanding the world and humans' place in it – is the foundation of Indigenous Australian philosophy.

The Dispossessed by Ursula Le Guin

We need artists and writers to imagine different ways of doing things, their possibilities and pitfalls. Le Guin, one of the great authors of all time, in my view, in this novel presents utopia/dystopia and more.

A Classless Society: Britain in the 1990s by Alwyn W. Turner

Grounded in the politics of the decade, the author sees that as shaping the culture – the Spice Girls fitted right in, 'Cool Britannia' was art all about the brand. If you were not there, it will help you understand your parents and teachers; if you were, will make you wince about how it all turned out.

Chapter 9: Recovering Space

The Book of Trespass by Nick Hayes

One of the founders of the Right to Roam movement sets out the case, and walks the walk, all across our privatised landscape, showing what we have lost, and what we can achieve with citizen science and watchful eyes.

All That is Solid by Danny Dorling
There are now more bedrooms per person than ever before in the UK. What we need to do is tackle the distribution and accessibility of housing. Dorling is one of the few commentators who does not say 'build, build, build'. And he is right.

Who Owns England? How We Lost Our Land and How to Take It Back by Guy Shrubsole
A compelling argument for land reform (one of my favourite phrases in the House of Lords, which makes the hereditary peers squirm), starting with a basic provision – transparency of ownership.

Chapter 10: Repairing the Broken

Sex at the Margins: Migration, Labour Markets and the Rescue Industry by Laura María Agustín
I have long been campaigning for the decriminalisation of sex work on the New Zealand model. Agustín places sex work as part of a far broader trend in the global economy that forces the marginalised, the immigrant, the dispossessed, to make commoditised performances of care.

The Naked Don't Fear the Water: An Underground Journey With Afghan Refugees by Matthieu Aikins
A powerful, personal account of one journalist's choice to journey as a refugee with his Afghan friend across Europe in 2016.

The Little Book of Prison: A Beginners Guide by Frankie Owens
I think it was Frankie himself who gave me a copy. It sits on my
shelf still. You never know when your life might demand it. Even if
you do not need its practical tips, it serves as an exposé of the
pointlessness of our carceral system.

Chapter 11: Rebalancing the World

The Storyteller's Daughter by Saira Shah
A memoir by the young British Afghan maker of the 2001 documentary *Beneath the Veil*, which told the story of women's lives under the
last-but-one Taliban regime, this gets under the skin of a place too
often seen only in the grainy footage of a killer drone about to strike.

Blood River: A Journey to Africa's Broken Heart by Tim Butcher
Reading this in 2008 sparked my continuing interest in the enormous, overwhelming tragedy of peoples never given a chance to find
stability. When I have been able to, I have been pursuing Congo
issues ever since, from sexual violence to children working in mines.
This is a classic crazy journey story. But one with a real purpose.

Ecocide: Kill the Corporation Before It Kills Us by David Whyte
I have worked closely with those campaigning to create an international crime of ecocide, securing the first parliamentary debate
on it soon after a new, carefully worked and deliverable legal definition was released. This book sets out the necessity for it, and the
way forward.

Chapter 12: Making Reparation

*Late Victorian Holocausts: El Niño Famines and the Making of the
Third World* by Mike Davis

A classic; the London Library copy is worn down almost to its bindings. As an explanation of how the Global South was under-developed (the process of colonial destruction that is still ongoing), this is hard to beat.

Insurgent Empire: Anticolonial Resistance and British Dissent by Priyamvada Gopal

We are often told that we cannot judge the past by the standards of the present. But from slavery to colonial exploitation, there were plenty of voices through recent centuries saying the exploitation was not acceptable. Priyamvada uncovers crucial history.

The Many-Headed Hydra: The Hidden History of the Revolutionary Atlantic by Peter Linebaugh and Marcus Rediker

There was strong, determined, creative resistance to the colonial projects, which fed ideas, and people, into struggles for freedom in the colonising states. This book makes the links and uncovers many voices that deserve to be remembered.

Colonialism and Modern Social Theory by Gurminder K. Bhambra and John Holmwood

A powerful – if quite technical – demonstration of the shared destructive error of liberal and Marxist thinking; the idea of a fixed, inevitable progress of history.

Notes

Introduction

1 Gerardo Ceballos et al., 'Accelerated modern human-induced species losses: Entering the sixth mass extinction', *Science Advances*, 19 June 2015, DOI: 10.1126/sciadv.140025

2 Y. M. Bar-On, R. Phillips and R. Milo, 'The biomass distribution on Earth', *Proceedings of the National Academy of Sciences*, 115 (25), 2018, 6506–6511, www.pnas.org/doi/abs/10.1073/pnas.1711842115

3 L. Greenspoon, et al., 'The global biomass of wild mammals', *Proceedings of the National Academy of Sciences*, 120 (10), 2023, e2204892120, www.pnas.org/doi/10.1073/pnas.2204892120

4 Bar-On et al., 'The biomass distribution on Earth'.

5 'The Obesity Paradox: An Excerpt from *Nourished Planet*', foodtank.com/news/2018/08/obesity-paradox-nourished-planet/

6 www.ukpol.co.uk/gordon-brown-1997-mansion-house-speech/

7 Fukuyama saw after the fall of the Berlin Wall the 'unabashed victory of economic and political liberalism'. Francis Fukuyama, 'The End of History? The National Interest', 16 (3), 1989, Center for the National Interest.

8 Chris Giles, 'Political optimism conceals a bleak outlook for Britain', *Financial Times*, 28 September 2017.

9 Katherine Richardson et al., 'Earth beyond six of nine planetary boundaries', *Science Advances*, 13 September 2023, www.science.org/doi/10.1126/sciadv.adh2458

10 Roisin O'Connor, 'Rachel Reeves says Labour does not want to represent people out of work', *Independent*, 17 March 2015.

Chapter 1: Decommodifying Time

1 Quoted in *Emma Goldman: A Documentary History of the American Years, Volume 1: Made for America, 1890-1901,* University of Illinois Press, 2008, p. 158.

2 'Births in England and Wales: 2021', Office for National Statistics, 9 August 2022, www.ons.gov.uk/peoplepopulationandcommunity/ birthsdeathsandmarriages/livebirths/bulletins/birthsummary tablesenglandandwales/2021

3 'Finland – Universal Basic Income Pilot', Wellbeing Economy Alliance, weall.org/resource/finland-universal-basic-income-pilot

Chapter 2: Education For All, For Free, For Life

1 www.nature.com/articles/s41599-021-00903-w

2 Anna N. Osiecka et al., 'Unpaid Work in Marine Science: A Snapshot of the Early-Career Job Market', *Frontiers in Marine Science*, 20 August 2021, doi.org/10.3389/fmars.2021.690163

3 Strochlic, Bynina, 'The Race to Save the World's Disappearing Languages: Every two weeks a language dies. Wikitongues wants to save them', *National Geographic*, April 16, 2018 www.nationalgeographic. com/culture/article/saving-dying-disappearing-languages-wikitongues-culture

4 G. Cajete, 'Native Science and Sustaining Indigenous Communities'. In M. Nelson and D. Shilling (Eds.), *Traditional Ecological Knowledge: Learning from Indigenous Practices for Environmental Sustainability*, Cambridge University Press pp. 15–26, DOI:10.1017/9781108552 998.003

5 www.vox.com/2014/8/21/6053187/cropland-map-food-fuel-animal-feed

6 Matthew Warke and Alice Butler-Warke, 'Portland stone: how a creamy British limestone became a symbol of empire and elitism', *The Conversation*, 30 July 2021, theconversation.com/portland-stone-

how-a-creamy-british-limestone-became-a-symbol-of-empire-and-elitism-163763

7 Carmen Aguila García et al., 'Fifth of UK universities' income comes from overseas students, figures show', *Guardian*, 14 July 2023, www.theguardian.com/education/2023/jul/14/overseas-students-uk-universities-income

Chapter 3: DIY Politics

1 Robert Pape, 'Deep, Divisive, Disturbing and Continuing: New Survey Shows Mainstream Support for Violence to Restore Trump Remains Strong', Chicago Project on Security and Threats, 2 January 2022, cpost.uchicago.edu/publications/deep_divisive_disturbing_and_continuing_new_survey_shows_maintream_support_for_violence_to_restore_trump_remains_strong/

2 Adam Bychawski, 'Revealed: Labour taking free staff from scandal-hit consulting firms The party has welcomed PricewaterhouseCoopers back to the fold even though Rachel Reeves called for it to be broken up,' *Open Democracy*, 6 June 2023, www.opendemocracy.net/en/labour-pwc-ey-big-four-natwest-hydrogen-keir-starmer-secondment-staff/

3 Natalie Bennett, 'Letter: It's time the UK had a written constitution', *Financial Times*, 22 September 2020, www.ft.com/content/034d31c3-005f-4eeb-b590-a6f9bc74b169

4 Robert Booth and Matthew Taylor, 'Prince Charles's "black spider memos" show lobbying at highest political level', *Guardian*, 13 May 2015, www.theguardian.com/uk-news/2015/may/13/prince-charles-black-spider-memos-lobbying-ministers-tony-blair

5 I worked with Eduoard Gaudot on the *Green European Journal* in 2023 to produce a series of articles exploring in much more detail the Green model of leadership: www.greeneuropeanjournal.eu/what-is-green-leadership/

Chapter 4: Restoring the Earth

1 S. M. Ghazani and A. G. Marangoni, 'Healthy Fats and Oils', *Elsevier Reference Module in Food* Science, 2016, doi.org/10.1016/B978-0-08-100596-5.00100-1, www.sciencedirect.com/science/article/pii/B97800 81005965001001

2 Emile A. Frison, 'From Uniformity to Diversity: A paradigm shift from industrial agriculture to diversified agroecological systems', iPES Food, 2016, www.ipes-food.org/_img/upload/files/UniformityToDiversity_FULL.pdf

3 Melissa C. Lott, '10 Calories in, 1 Calorie Out – The Energy We Spend on Food', *Scientific American*, 11 August 2011, blogs.scientificamerican.com/plugged-in/10-calories-in-1-calorie-out-the-energy-we-spend-on-food/

4 FAO, 'Small family farmers produce a third of the world's food', 23 April 2021, www.fao.org/news/story/en/item/1395127/icode/

5 'Hedgerows: the unsung heroes of nature', hedgelink.org.uk/campaign/national-hedgerow-week/about-hedges, 2023

6 'Why meadows matter', 24 May 2017, Royal Botanic Gardens Kew, www.kew.org/read-and-watch/meadows-matter

7 David R. Montgomery, *Dirt: The Erosion of Civilisations*, University of California Press, 2008, p. 174.

8 'The State of Britain's Hedgehogs 2022', Natural Biodiversity Network, 2 March 2022, nbn.org.uk/news/the-state-of-britains-hedgehogs-2022/

9 Samuel Turvey, *Witness to Extinction: How We Failed to Save the Yangtze River Dolphin*, Oxford University Press, 2009

10 Julia Blackburn, *Thin Paths*, Jonathan Cape: London, 2011, p. 205.

11 Tim Dee, *Four Fields*, Random House: London, 2013, p. 42.

12 This has been described as a 'dark episode for Sheffield', when thousands of healthy street trees were unnecessarily felled, the High Court was misled, and councillors were dishonest with the public as the police were enlisted by the Labour council to enforce novel interpretations of anti-trade-union legislation. Helen Pidd, 'Sheffield city council behaved dishonestly in street trees row, inquiry finds', *Guardian*, 6 March 2023, theguardian.com/uk-news/2023/mar/06/

sheffield-city-council-behaved-dishonestly-in-street-trees-row-inquiry-finds

13 Roger S. Ulrich, 'View Through a Window May Influence Recovery from Surgery', *Science*, 224 (4647), 1984.

14 Arnold J. Wilkins, 'Looking at buildings can actually give people headaches – here's how', *The Conversation*, 1 June 2017, theconversation.com/looking-at-buildings-can-actually-give-people-headaches-heres-how-74565

15 F. Lutzoni, M. D. Nowak, M. E. Alfaro et al., 'Contemporaneous radiations of fungi and plants linked to symbiosis', *Nature Communications* 9 (5451), 21 December 2018, doi.org/10.1038/s41467-018-07849-9

Chapter 5: The People's Economy

1 'The Impacts of Clothing', Traid, September 2018, traid.org.uk/wp-content/uploads/2018/09/impacts_of_clothing_factsheet_23percent.pdf

2 Alix Smidman, Elfredah Kavin-Alerechi and Gideon Sarping, 'UK's second-hand clothing pollutes African nations', *The Ferret*, 27 October 2022, theferret.scot/uk-second-hand-clothing-pollutes-african-nations

3 Esther Batt, 'Flaws in Fast Fashion', *UCL Institute for Sustainable Resources*, www.ucl.ac.uk/bartlett/sustainable/news/2022/apr/flaws-fast-fashion-atacama-desert-dumping-ground

4 Chavie Lieber, 'Why fashion brands destroy billions' worth of their own merchandise every year', *Vox*, 17 September 2018, www.vox.com/the-goods/2018/9/17/17852294/fashion-brands-burning-merchandise-burberry-nike-h-and-m

5 'How many Earths? How many countries?', www.overshootday.org/how-many-earths-or-countries-do-we-need/

6 Tim Callen, 'Gross Domestic Product: An Economy's All', *IMF*, www.imf.org/en/Publications/fandd/issues/Series/Back-to-Basics/gross-domestic-product-GDP

Chapter 6: Controlling the Money

1 'City of London Funds', cityofLondon.gov.uk, 26 September 2023, www.cityoflondon.gov.uk/about-us/budgets-spending/city-of-london-funds

2 Andrew Laing, 'Costing Corruption and Efficiency Losses from Weak PFM Systems', *IMF*, 3 April 2023, blog-pfm.imf.org/en/pfmblog/2023/04/costing-corruption-and-efficiency-losses-from-weak-pfm-systems

3 'Fact Check-Video claiming BlackRock and Vanguard "own all the biggest corporations in the world" is missing context', Reuters Fact Check, 20 April 2022, www.reuters.com/article/factcheck-business-investment-idUSL2N2WI1K4

4 'Exchanges carrying 3 times more carbon reserves than can be burned under Paris', *Carbon Tracker*, 23 June 2022, carbontracker.org/stock-exchanges-carrying-3-times-more-reserves-than-can-be-burned-under-paris/

5 Terry Chan and Alexandra Dimitrijevic, 'Global Debt Leverage: Is a Great Reset Coming?', S&P Global, www.spglobal.com/en/research-insights/featured/special-editorial/look-forward/global-debt-leverage-is-a-great-reset-coming

6 Becky Malone, '99.5% of Government Covid debt has been matched by so called Bank of England "Money Printing"', New Economics Foundation, 25 October 2021, neweconomics.org/2021/10/99-5-of-government-covid-debt-has-been-matched-by-so-called-bank-of-england-money-printing

Chapter 7: Enabling Wellbeing

1 'International comparisons of life expectancy', Health Foundation, 17 April 2022, www.health.org.uk/evidence-hub/health-inequalities/international-life-expectancy

2 'UK health system comes out on top in new report', NHS England, 14 July 2017, www.england.nhs.uk/2017/07/uk-health-system-comes-out-on-top-in-new-report/

3 Peter Russell, 'Hospital Waiting List Breaches 7.5 Million for First Time', Medscape UK, 11 August 2023, www.medscape.co.uk/view-article/hospital-waiting-list-breaches-7-5-million-first-time-2023a1000iij

4 Matt Dathan, 'NHS hires more foreign doctors than total medical school intake', *The Times*, April 6, 2023, www.thetimes.co.uk/article/nhs-hires-more-foreign-doctors-than-total-medical-school-intake-znjc2rk2

5 Registration data reports, Nursing & Midwifery Council, www.nmc.org.uk/about-us/reports-and-accounts/registration-statistics/

6 'The City Fund', 26 September 2023, www.cityoflondon.gov.uk/about-us/budgets-spending/city-of-london-funds

7 John Lister, 'The History of Privatisation', The Lowdown, 16 March 2020, lowdownnhs.info/analysis/long-read/the-history-of-privatisation-second-in-a-series-by-john-lister/

8 'A chat every other day keeps dementia at bay?', Alzforum, 31 August 2022, www.alzforum.org/news/conference-coverage/chat-every-other-day-keeps-dementia-bay

9 Daniel A. Rodriguez, *The Right to Live in Health: Medical Politics in Postindependence Havana*, University of North Carolina Press, 2020.

Chapter 9: Recovering Space

1 Steve Robson, 'Government becomes biggest rail operator for first time in decades as TransPennine Express loses contract', *iNews*, 11 May 2023, inews.co.uk/news/government-biggest-rail-operator-first-time-decades-transpennine-express-2333229

2 Joe Bradbury, 'The housing deficit in 2023', *Housing Association Magazine*, 19 January 2023, www.hamag.co.uk/The-housing-deficit-in-2023

3 Benjamin Kentish, 'Forty percent of homes sold under Right to Buy now in the hands of private landlords, new analysis reveals', *Independent*, 8 December 2017, www.independent.co.uk/news/uk/

politics/right-to-buy-homes-sold-private-landlords-latest-figures-rent-a8098126.html

4 Gareth Davies, Charles Boutaud, Hazel Sheffield, Emma Youle, 'Revealed: The Thousands of Public Spaces Lost to the Council Funding Crisis', *The Bureau of Investigative Journalism*, 4 March 2019, www.thebureauinvestigates.com/stories/2019-03-04/sold-from-under-you

5 Nick Hayes, *The Book of Trespass: Crossing the Lines that Divide Us*, Bloomsbury: London, 2020.

6 D. B Hayhow, et al., *The State of Nature 2016*, DOI:10.13140/RG.2.2.12520.26882

Chapter 10: Repairing the Broken

1 'Prison: the facts', Prison Reform Trust, prisonreformtrust.org.uk/wp-content/uploads/2023/06/prison_the_facts_2023.pdf

2 Calum Rosie, 'Private Prisons have shown a Lax Approach to Human Rights', EachOther.org, 26 April 2021 eachother.org.uk/private-prisons-have-shown-a-lax-approach-to-human-rights/

3 Justice Committee, 'Women in Prisons', House of Commons Committee report, 26 July 2022, publications.parliament.uk/pa/cm5803/cmselect/cmjust/265/report.html

4 'What is immigration detention?', Avid, aviddetention.org.uk/immigration-detention/what-immigration-detention

5 Rachel Makinson, 'LASPO: How a near-decade of legal air cuts has affected Britain's most vulnerable', *Lawyer Monthly*, 26 August 2021, www.lawyer-monthly.com/2021/08/laspo-how-a-near-decade-of-legal-aid-cuts-has-affected-britains-most-vulnerable/

6 D. Clark, 'Resource department expenditure limit (RDEL) of criminal and civil legal aid in England and Wales from 2005/06 to 2021/22', Statista, 20 July 2023, www.statista.com/statistics/1098628/legal-aid-spending-in-england-and-wales/

7 'PAC: MoJ's "meagre" ambition to fix breaking CJS as year-plus waits for serious criminal trials more than trebles', 9 March 2022, committees.parliament.uk/committee/127/public-accounts-

committee/news/161538/pac-mojs-meagre-ambition-to-fix-breaking-cjs-as-yearplus-waits-for-serious-criminal-trials-more-than-trebles/

8 'From harm to hope: A 10-year drugs plan to cut crime and save lives', Gov.uk, 29 April 2022, www.gov.uk/government/publications/from-harm-to-hope-a-10-year-drugs-plan-to-cut-crime-and-save-lives/from-harm-to-hope-a-10-year-drugs-plan-to-cut-crime-and-save-lives

Chapter 11: Rebalancing the World

1 John Burn-Murdoch, 'Why are Americans dying so young?', *Financial Times*, 30 March 2023, www.ft.com/content/653bbb26-8a22-4db3-b43d-c34a0b774303

2 'Climate Change and War: How US Military Emissions Factor into Costs of War and Shape Military Policy', *Democracy Now*, 17 March 2023, www.democracynow.org/2023/3/17/climate_change_war_how_us_military

3 John Reed, 'The king's money: Thailand divided over the $40bn question', *Financial Times*, 13 October 2020.

4 'The Most Reputable Countries in the World', Knoema.com, 11 October 2022, knoema.com/infographics/axgsdxc/the-most-reputable-countries-in-the-world

5 Robert Burns, 'Billions spent on Afghan army ultimately benefitted Taliban', *Associated Press*, 17 August 2021, apnews.com/article/joe-biden-army-taliban-995b069a9008690582cb34f4cacd8515

Chapter 12: Making Reparation

1 Ernest Aryeetey and Zenia Lewis, 'African Land Grabbing: Whose Interests Are Served?', Brookings, 25 June 2010, www.brookings.edu/articles/african-land-grabbing-whose-interests-are-served/

2 'How many Earths? How many countries?', Earth Overshoot Day, www.overshootday.org/how-many-earths-or-countries-do-we-need/, accessed 9 October 2023

3 James H. Sweet, 'Is History History?: Identity Politics and Teleologies of the Present', American Historical Association: Perspectives on History, 17 August 2022, www.historians.org/research-and-publications/perspectives-on-history/september-2022/is-history-history-identity-politics-and-teleologies-of-the-present

4 Harriet Sherwood, 'Indians in the trenches: voices of forgotten army are finally to be heard', *Guardian*, 27 October 2018, www.theguardian.com/world/2018/oct/27/armistice-centenary-indian-troops-testimony-sacrifice-british-library

5 Gopal, Priyamvada, *Insurgent Empire: Anticolonial Resistance and British Dissent,* Verso, 2019, pp. 60, 88.

6 Campaign for Nuclear Disarmament, '£205 billion: the cost of Trident', cnduk.org/resources/205-billion-cost-trident.

Index

Supporters

Unbound is the world's first crowdfunding publisher, established in 2011.

We believe that wonderful things can happen when you clear a path for people who share a passion. That's why we've built a platform that brings together readers and authors to crowdfund books they believe in – and give fresh ideas that don't fit the traditional mould the chance they deserve.

This book is in your hands because readers made it possible. Everyone who pledged their support is listed below. Join them by visiting unbound. com and supporting a book today.

Jo A
Tamsin Abbott
Daimon Ablett
Martha
   Adam-Bushell
Neil Adams
Jennifer Agricola
David Albone
Julze Alejandre
Nicholas Alexander
Hannah Allbrooke
Caroline Allen
Charlie Allen
Kelly Allen
George Allison
Stuart Allison
Keith Anderson
Professor Alison
   Anderson
Chris Andrew
Gavin Andrews

Sabrina Artus
Bob Ashwood
Nigel Atkin
Thomas Atkin
Richard Atkins
Lindsey Atkinson
Tricia Austin
Sue Avery
Melinda Balatoni
Laurence Baldwin
Andrea Barbieri
Caroline Barker
Debbie Barnes
Pamela, Neil, Maddie
   and Izzy Barnes
Anthony Barnett
Richard Barrington
Thomas Barron
Harry Bartholomew
Jane Baston
Suswati Basu

Lynne Bateman
Rowena Baxter
Peter Bayliss
Dorothée Bechtloff
Johann Beckford
Chris Beddoes
Alex Bellars
Andrew Bennett
Andrew Clive Bennett
F Bennett
Kareena Amara
   Bennett
Philip Allen Bennett
Penny Bennetts
Alex Benstead
Rachel Bentham
Sian Berry
Andrew Best
Nic Best
Jean Betteridge
Toby Bettridge

Stephanie Betts
Su Billington
Ursula Bilson Haines
Carol Birch
Keary Birch
Nicola Blackwell
Joanne Blair
Jane Blake
Martin Blake
Mimi Blanksby
Philip Blunt
Emily Blyth
Nigel Boatman
Emilie Bonnevay
A Bortlik
Katy Boyce
Colin Boyle
Peter Boyle
Phil Brachi
Sean Brady
Chris Bragg
Clive Bramley
Anna Brandon
Nigel Brazier
Marie Brett
Valerie Briginshaw
Graham Briscoe
Emma Britton
Lucy Brooker
Lorna Brooks
Paul Brown
Matt Browne
Robert Buckman
Emma Bullard
Rodney Burton
Mike Butcher
Natalie Buttriss
Marcus Cain
Anne Calderbank

Paul Campbell
Angela Cant
Dr Howard Carlton
Tracy Carter
Roger Cartwright
Debbie Casey
Norm Cassidy
Jamie Cave
Rachel Chamberlain
    Duerden
Connor Chapman
Gillian Charters
David Chaytor
John Cherry
Isobel Chester
Victoria Chester
Tchiyiwe T Chihana
Heather Clare
Ian and Helen Clark
Paul Clark
Jeremy Clarke
Phillip Clarke
Ian Clarkson
Molly Clayton
Joe Clear
David Clegg
Darren & Katie
    Clementson-Lee
Ant Clifford
Dilys Cluer
Janet Cobb
Alix Cockcroft
David Collier
Andrew Collins
David Collins
Belinda Coney
Kathryn Cook
Stephen Cook
Tessa Coombes

Gill Coombs
Louise Cooper
Katherine Ann Cope
Gi Copley
Nicola Corrigan
Paul Corry
Melina Costelloe
Martin Coule
Gillian Coyle
Ellie Crane
R Crane
Sally Cranfield
Helen Crawley
John Cresswell-Plant
    in Memory of my
    wife Katie
Liz Crix
Sarah Louise Croke
Bev Cross
Michael Culverhouse
Robin Curtis
Meryn Cutler
Gareth Dalglish
Michael Darke
Laura Davenport
Ivor Davies
Philip Davies
Sally Davies
Thomas Daw
Emma Dawnay
Thomas Day
Maya de Souza
Charlie & Kasia Dean
Julian Dean
Chris Denton
David Derbyshire
Dominic Devlin
Pallavi Devulapalli
Diana

Jim Dignan
Dave Dixey
J E Dixon
Johnny Dixon
David Donoghue
Mark Donovan
Jonny Douglas
Simon Dowling
Linda Downey
Claudia Drake
Kat Driscoll
Katy Duke
Paul Duley
Stewart and Maja
    Dunn
Carolyn Dwyer
Dave Eagle
Lynne Maria East
George Edgar
Shaun Edgar
Laura Edie
Chris Edmond
Brian Edwards
Matt Edwards
Marieanne Elliot
Dominic Elson
David Ely
June Emerson
Robert Ensch
Carol Evans
James Evans
Rachel Evans
Paul-Enguerrand Fady
R Fairbank
David Farbey
Sally Fereday
Matt Firth
Martin Fisher
Paul Fisher

Stephen Fisher
James Fitt
Joshua Fleck
Bianca Folkers
Chris Fosten
Elaine Francis
Tom Franklin
Andree Frieze
Jonathan Frost
Julie Froud
Rhys Fullerton
Kerena Fussell
Samantha Gaist
Emma Garnett
Cah Garstang
Lucy Gee
Ray Georgeson
Janet Georgiou
Stephen Gibbons
Joshua Gladwin
Gwyneth Godding
Olga Gomez-Cash
Paul Goodison
Fred Gough
Evelyn Goulden
Kas Graham
Claire Grant
John Grayling
Good Green
Yasmin Gregory
Paul Grime
Tim Gripton
Martin Grocock
Ingrid Gubbay
Julie Guihen
Tracey Guise
Claire Guyver
Scott Haig
Cris Hale

John Philip Hall
Louise Hall
Wayne Hallam
Jette Halling
Lou Hamilton
Peter Hampson
Sheelagh Handy
Elizabeth Hanson
Rebecca Harcourt
Clare Hardy
Adam Harper
Ian Harris
Josh Harris
Joshua Harris
Kalen Harris
Toni Harrison
Jamie Hart
Rob Hart
Nick Hartley
Anne Kristin
    Hartmann
Ian Hartwright
Luke Harvey-Ingram
Alison Hawdale
Anthony Hay
Simon Haynes
Andrew Hearse
Sheila Hedges
Tony Henderson
Stephen Wm Hesketh
Amanda Hickling
Celia Hickson
David Higgins
Nate Higgins
Nigel Hiley
Sally Hilton
Nicolas Hindley
Richard Hixson
James Hobbs

Michael Hodges
Kathryn Hodgson
Rachel Holland
Ollie Holliday
Kerenza Hood
Jane Hopkins
Louise Houghton
Alan Houldcroft
Walter Houston
David Howdle-Smith
Ashton Howick
Leo Huckvale
Libby Hudson
Owen Hughes
Nigel Hunt
Lee Huntbach
James Hydes
Steve Hynd
Patricia Ingram
Steven Jacobs
Paul James
Nicola J James
    BSc, PhD
Chris Jarvis
Mike Jelfs
Finn Jensen
Jim Jepps
Christopher Jerrey
Douglas Johnson
Rachel Johnson
Dave Jones
Hugh Jones
Iolo Jones
Peter Jones
Thomas Ythan Jones
Andrew Jordan
Stephen Jordan
Jacqueline Jung
Sheridan Kates

Robin Keech
Jamie Kendrick
Summer Kennedy
Thady Kennedy
Martha Kenyon
Jonathan Edward
    Kershaw
Dan Kieran
Tom Killick
Jillian King
Matt King
Julian King-Salter
Jamie Kingston
Alice Knight
Michael Knight
Lars Kramm
John Krebs
Charlotte Lafferty
Anthony Lamb
Steve Lambert
Jane Langley
Sue Lansbury
Nigel Lax
Carolyn Leather
Joe Lemmer
Jon Leopold
Evelyn Leslie
Karen Lewing
Erskine Lewis
Jonathon Liston
Grace Lockrobin
Steve Loft
John Logan
Andrea Monica Longos
Mike Lowe
Caroline Lucas
Ursula Lucas
Donald Lunan
David Lungley

Jen Lunn
Ben M
Adrian Mabe
Sue Mallender
James A Man
Jessina Ann Manjaly
Elizabeth Mansfield
Laura Manston
Simon Marchant
Shiona Marsh
John Marshall
Kim Marshall
Prof. Julia
    Martin-Ortega
Craig Maylor
Claire McIlvenna
Sophie McInnes
Robert McIntosh
Emily McIvor
Dr. Stephen
    McKeever
Alan McKinnon
Carol McQuire
Stephanie McVeigh
Anthony Meadowcroft
Andrew Melville
Members of Hilling-
    don Green Party
Emma Menhinnitt
Ute Michel
Jeni Miles
Edward Milford
Eleanor Miller
Judy Miller
Rob Miller
Chris Millman
Nadia Mitchell
John Mitchinson
Matty Mitford

Andi Mohr
Jenny Moran
Elizabeth Mordue
Patrick Morgan
Fionnuala Morris
Alex Morss
Andy Morton
Rosalyn Mott
Anne Mountjoy
Josie Muller
David Murray
Sam Murray
Miralem Mustafić
Junaid Nasir
Carlo Navato
John New
Philip Newton
Jacqui Jewell Nicholls
Sue Nicholls
Roger Nisbet
Kirsty Noble
Katharine Norbury
Lloyd North
Chantelle Norton
Jon Nott
Cllr Rob Nunney
Emily O'Brien
Mike O'Day
Tim O'Leary
James Ockenden
Michelle Oldale
Lt Col Baroness
    Catherine Jade
    Olusoga
Christina ONeill
Robert Orange
Organisation for
    Responsible
    Businesses

Rick Ormrod
Fernando Orus
Guy Otten
The Outsider
Marianne Overton
    MBE
Jenneth Parker
Sam Parkinson
Neil Parsons
Steve Parsons
Shahram Parvin
Maciej Pawlik
Martin Pearcy
Hugo Perks
Anthony Peter
Jenny Peters
Remco Peters
Lisa Pettifer
Bridget Petty
Sarah Phibbs
Christopher Phillips
Debby Plummer
Zack Polanski
Justin Pollard
Rebecca Prentice
Anna Presswell
Dawn Preston
Ivana Prica
Colin Pritchard
Julie Radford
Daniel Rafferty
Serena Ralston
Katrina Ramage
Laura Ramsey
Nick and Jan Reed
Darrin Reeves
Jason Reeves
Rachel Reeves
Betsy Reid

Julia Rennert
David Reynolds
Helena Richards
Rosalind Ridout
Kelly Rigden
Pamela Ritchie
Anne Rix
Mike Robbins
Carolyn Joanne
    Roberts
Tony Roberts
Scott Robertson
Caroline Robertson-
    Brown
Pauline Robinson
William Robinson
Justina Robson
Sandie Rose
Duncan Ross
Mandy Rossi
David Rowe
Mark Rudd
Carole Rust
Janet Rutter
Jo Salter
John Saunders
Shelley Saunders
Linda Sawyer
Carol Sayles
Alice Scarlett
Francisca Sconce
Manda Scott
Norman Scott
Jessie Scoullar
Daniel Sewell
Mike Shaw
Siobhan K M Shea
Brian Shepherd
Meg Shepherd-Foster

Frank Sheridan
Mandy Sherwood
Oliver Sidorczuk
Paul Simpson
Sally Sines
Sarah Skeels
Joe Slater
Anthony Slaughter
Matthew Smith
John Smout
Leeds Solar
Ann Southworth-
    Phelan
P Speed
Cord Spilker
Sabrina Spilker
Adrian Spurrell
Graham Stacey
Susan Stainer
Andi Stamp
Ann Stapleton
Jacquie Steel
Alan Steele
Will Steer
Tobias Steiner
Claire Stephenson
Aaron Sterniczky
Evelyn Stevens
Nicola Stewart
Ronald Stewart
Philly Stock
Joern Strueber,
    Darmstadt
Krzysztof Strug
Ric Swann
Joseph Swift
Cathryn Symons
SURGAT__
Christine Talmage

David Tannahill
Lorna Taylor
Stephen Taylor
The Greyhound
    Community
Matthew Thomas
Stephen Thompson
Frank Thomson
Jessica Tickell
Helen Tiley
Fredi Tobler
Ewan Tomeny
Caroline Tomes
Friendship Tour
Lindsay Trevarthen
Stephanie Trotter,
    OBE
Chloe Turner
Jo Turner
Paul Urwin
Natasha Usher
Jan Van den Bergh
Fabio van den Ende
Alex Varley-Winter
Sarah Vaughan
Ann Von Essen
Elizabeth Waight
Hannah R Wakley
Chris Walford
Richard Walker
Jack Wallington
Sarah Walpole
Chris Ward
Eamonn Ward
Rose Mary
    Warrington
Eve Waterside
John Waterworth
Olli Watkins

Nicola Watson
David W. Weaver
E Webb
Elen Webb
Becca Wedge-
    Roberts
Joan E West
Kathryn Wheeler
Caroline Whitaker
Paul Whitaker
Kate White
Thomas White
Jim Whitehead
Daisy Wiles Holt
Lucy Wilkins
Sandy Wilkinson
David Willetts
Barbara Williams
Carwyn Williams
Chris Williams
Dr Rob Williams
Huw Williams
Katherine May
    Williams
Zoe Williams
Kev Willis
Louise Wills
Daniel Wilson
Nik Windle
James Windridge
Sarah Windrum
Catherine Wood
Sally Wood
Peter Woolstenholmes
Craig Wright
Georgina Wright
Graham Wroe
Kate Yates
Jacek Zmarzlik